Beyond Welfare and Full Employment

Beyond Welfare and Full Employment

The Economics of Optimal
Employment without Inflation

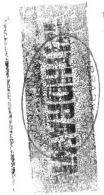

Dean A. Worcester, Jr.
University of Washington

Lexington Books
D.C. Heath and Company
Lexington, Massachusetts
Toronto   London

This book is dedicated to my father

Dean A. Worcester

whose life communicates a love
of truth-seeking and
concern for others

Contents

List of Figures   ix

List of Tables   xi

Preface   xiii

Introduction   xv

Part I   **Unemployment in Prosperity: The Long View and Recent Statistics**   1

Chapter 1   An Unsolved Problem of Modern Economics: Interdependence of Unemployment, Welfare Programs, and Inflation   3

Chapter 2   Basis for a Theory of Unemployment: Analysis of Preferences and Income Opportunities   21

Chapter 3   United States Welfare Programs and Work Incentives   39

Part II   **Analysis and a Positive Program**   65

Chapter 4   Individual Decisions and Social Welfare: Toward a Theory of Optimal Employment   67
Appendix
A Factor Mispricing Theory of Unemployment   85

Chapter 5   Policies to Equalize Private and Social Costs of Labor   99

Chapter 6   Size of Welfare Payments and Financing   113

Chapter 7   Impacts of Optimal Employment Policy on Governmental Regulation of Enterprise   139

Notes   147

Index   153

About the Author   157

List of Figures

1–1	Labor Force Trends	9
1–2	Trend in Income Distribution: 1929–68	11
1–3	Social Welfare Expenditures	13
1–4	Response to Depression and Response to Prosperity	15
2–1	Some Income Opportunities	24
2–2	Income Possibility Lines for Six Groups of Low Income Families, 1965	27
2–3	Income Possibility Lines and Indifference Curves for Six Groups of Low Income Families, 1965	29
2–4	Effect of Nonwork Income on Hours of Work Desired under Cobb-Douglas Assumptions: Wages Variable	33
2–5	Predicted Response to Benefit Payments at Constant Wage Rates	35
3–1	Nonwork Income: Tax Effects versus Absence of Work Ethic	41
3–2	Analysis of OASI	44
3–3	Further Analysis of OASI	47
3–4	Unemployment Insurance Benefits in Wisconsin, 1967	49
3–5	Analysis of Public Assistance	51
3–6	A Family Assistance Plan	59
4–1	Life Cycle Employment Under Optimal Conditions	70
4–2	Social and Private Costs of Unemployment	73
4A–1	A General Equilibrium Analysis of Unemployment	89
5–1	Position Relative to Labor Force: Employment	106
6–1	Effects of a Property-Type Welfare Tax	119
6–2	$1000 Demogrant and Welfare Tax	123
6–3	Low Income Potential: $1000 Demogrant	128
6–4	Break-Even Income: $1000 Demogrant	129
6–5	High Income: $1000 Demogrant	130
6–6	$2500 Demogrant and Welfare Tax	133
6–7	Low Income: $2500 Demogrant	135
6–8	High Income: $2500 Demogrant	136

List of Tables

2–1   Hours Worked and Income Received from Work and Nonwork Sources by Low Income Families: 1965   27

2–2   Weekly Hours Worked in May 1970   38

3–1   Effect of Minimum Wages on Teenage Unemployment Rates   56

6–1   Estimated Costs and Benefits of $1000 Demogrant for Ten Income Levels: 1969   124

6–2   Estimated Costs and Benefits of a $2500 Demogrant for Ten Income Levels: 1969   132

Preface

The primary purpose of this book is theoretical. It attempts to show that the macroeconomic problems of unemployment and inflation are the result of contracting in labor markets where the costs that employers must pay for manpower, and the net gains received by potential workers from becoming employed, are systematically distorted. Our hope is that the shortcomings can be overcome when they are understood.

The secondary purpose of this book is to spell out the practical, policy-oriented implications of the theoretical analysis. They are of the first magnitude. To that end specific proposals are suggested in the final chapters to describe one way whereby the present welfare system can be transformed and generalized so as to reduce unemployment and feelings of alienation, and to provide more stable prices by improving the functioning of labor markets.

The initial chapter is devoted to the historical record that has produced the present crisis and opportunities. This might not be necessary if only professional economists were addressed here. But it is hoped that intellectuals outside the economics profession as well as students in their second or third course in economics will want to learn from this book. These readers are not likely to be acquainted with the record of unemployment, participation rates, growth and welfare expenditures, nor with the comparisons of economies that are summarized in chapter 1. Nor are they acquainted with the simple but powerful techniques explained in chapter 2 and utilized extensively in chapters 3, 4, 5, and 6.

Chapter 3 shows why welfare programs have tended to grow as rapidly in times of prosperity as in times of depression and why they have tended to be socially divisive rather than serving their intended purpose of holding society together by caring for the disadvantaged. Chapter 4 presents a theory of unemployment that, in a sense, turns Keynesian theory on its head and gives promise of policies that utilize welfare payments to carry us beyond the fuzzy concept of "full" employment to "optimal" employment. Professional economists may wish to go directly to the Appendix of chapter 4 for a more refined analysis. Chapter 5 presents a positive program for optimal employment without inflation. Methods of financing the system presented in chapter 5 are considered in chapter 6 and additional aspects of the suggested policies are sketched in chapter 7.

The basic ideas presented here were conceived during a brief respite from my research on externality problems. As it happened, I was in Bontoc, a rather primitive town in the Philippine mountains. The first effort to work out the basic ideas was presented as my presidential address to the Western Economic Association in 1968. The reception was enthusiastic by a few, but was, in general, bitterly disappointing to me. The disappointment led to a great deal of effort, discussion with many individuals, much rethinking.

I cannot justly determine those to whom I owe the greater debts of gratitude. Henry Wan should be mentioned first. More than any other he saw merit in what I attempted in my address and gave substantial encouragement at the time. I was not able to use the rather elaborate research plan that he outlined then and the present work no doubt suffers as a consequence, but I am most grateful to him. I am especially grateful to Robert J. Lampman whose detailed and careful reading has been invaluable, and to John S. McGee who also took the hard and careful look that is so helpful. Robert L. Bish, Thomas E. Borcherding, and Roger L. Miller read the whole manuscript and generously offered useful suggestions. C. Michael Rahm, Judith G. Thornton, and Richard W. Parks contributed useful insights related to chapters 4 and 5. Every effort has been made to benefit from the wisdom of these scholars and others who over the years have discussed these matters with me. But I did not adopt all of their suggestions and errors of commission and omission no doubt remain. They are my responsibility.

Introduction

Perhaps the great brute fact of the first half of the 1970s is acceptance of the idea that each person in the United States should enjoy a minimum income whether or not he is thought to deserve it according to some ethical standard. President Nixon, regarded by many as a conservative, has been the strongest proponent of action now to institute a minimum income for all families with children. Virtually no one attacks the idea of a minimum.

The level of minimum income proposed by President Nixon is not modest by international standards. He proposes an amount which is the equivalent of more than $2,400 annually for a family of four. This is about six times the average family income in Manila, where poverty is less grinding than in many other places in the world. It is above the average for Castro's Cuba, Allende's Chile, Sadat's Egypt. Still, the $2,400 minimum has been criticized as inadequate. Some elected United States congressmen have argued that the minimum should be $6,500 for a family.

A policy watershed will be reached if Congress passes the president's proposal. It will establish something like the extended family system, or tribal system of the past, for the 200 million plus people of a large multiracial nation. It will come full circle to the collective systems of the past which were largely abandoned when the idea of progress based on the rise of individual incentive, increased mobility, and self-reliance was accepted.

The revival is not without precedent. It is foreshadowed by poor laws, complicated welfare systems, and plans such as the comprehensive but short-lived, nineteenth-century Speenhamland system in a few English counties.

Guaranteed minimum incomes can bring frustration and failure if they sap our productive strength or leave us militarily naked to our enemies. But this is not a necessary result.

One object of this book is to show how constructively revolutionary the minimum income idea can be. It can harmonize individual freedom with social cooperation in a growing, people-oriented economy. It need not reduce the impulse to work. But it can eliminate the fearful drive for expansion simply to provide employment by clarifying the social function of work as service to others and by moderating anxiety about work as a source of income to the worker.

Remarkably, a guaranteed minimum income policy can also place *downward* pressures on prices while bringing us to optimal employment.

It is hard to keep a constant perspective while thinking about these matters. At times the analysis may strike the reader as being novel, exciting, even revolutionary because it brings together three areas of analysis and policy that are usually treated in isolation from each other. But the formal analysis used is simple and each logical step is a modest one. My greatest concern is that the level and style of the exposition does not obscure whatever merit the present work has.

A new approach to the persistently crisis-ridden issues of unemployment, poverty, inflation and alienation can avoid neither bruising contact with partisan advocates of existing programs and procedures, nor scorn from believers in ideologies that require total displacement our social system. Those who have built and who administer modern programs designed to combat unemployment and the other consequences of inadequate labor markets may feel that their enormous efforts are too little appreciated. But dedicated as those efforts have been, it must be admitted that the problems persist virtually unabated as causes of social discontent.

Some critics believe that high levels of military spending are necessary to avoid heavy unemployment in Western nations. They see this as wasteful at best, and at worst, terribly destructive. The Marxist position, which is accepted by many intellectuals around the world, predicts ultimate disaster for the West because their analysis makes employment contingent upon an impossible perpetual expansion of markets to make up for the deficiency of labor markets within the West. One does not have to agree with these views to find many expenditures which, although wasteful in themselves, are undertaken or subsidized by government and justified by the belief that they create additional employment, and/or growth.

Recently environmentalists have challenged this kind of thinking, but have been careful not to face the unemployment-creating aspect of their proposals head on. Instead, the specter of universal death is raised as the alternative to acceptance of their programs.

If this book's analysis is correct no need exists for any program whose purpose is solely to increase employment. Unemployment will not result from reduced government expenditures nor by the abandonment of government-subsidized private expenditure, provided that the necessary adjustments are made in labor markets. By the same token, there will be no need for tariffs, import quotas, and other blockages to efficient resource use in order to "provide jobs."

The theoretical analysis presented here involves welfare payments in an essential way. However, it should be understood that the book is not directed primarily toward a "solution" of the "poverty problem." I think that a solution is in fact offered, but it is an incidental aspect of the analysis.

Welfare benefits play an essential role primarily because they make visible and concrete vital social costs which were more informal, hidden, and "within the family" in former times. In a broad sense, welfare costs are fundamental to labor market inadequacies. The fact that a large part of welfare costs are governmentally funded and organized is an important, perhaps even necessary, precondition to an improvement in labor markets. It creates the possibility of mobilizing such costs so as to repair the shortcomings of labor markets while preserving and strengthening the income assistance offered by such programs.

This policy possibility is the result of the analysis, and it is developed to some extent in the final chapters. But the central effort is the analysis.

**Part I
Unemployment in Prosperity:
The Long View
and Recent Statistics**

1

An Unsolved Problem of Modern Economies: Interdependence of Unemployment, Welfare Programs, and Inflation

The Basic Problem

Unemployment, welfare programs, and inflation arise from the same base and are interconnected. They cannot be, in the last analysis, fruitfully examined separately because single-minded policies formed to alleviate particular problems in one area often have unexpected and unpleasant consequences in the other two.

Improved insight can liberate policy from disappointments and frustrations. The first section of this book describes the interconnections among the three areas and, hopefully, gives insight. A radical revision of U.S. income security programs is advanced in the final section to show how it may be possible to provide basic income security in such a way as to enhance output and virtually eliminate unemployment simultaneously with the removal of inflationary pressures.

Unemployment is defined here as it is by the U.S. Bureau of Labor Statistics. Briefly, a person is unemployed if he is: (1) willing to work, (2) able to work, (3) actively seeking work, and (4) unable to find work.

A key element of the definition of unemployment is the "participation rate." It defines the size of the labor force which, by United States definition, includes those who are at work in addition to the unemployed. The size of the labor force and the number unemployed is calculated from data collected from interviews.

There is a large subjective element in the United States conception of its labor force and rate of its unemployment. The individual interviewed is the primary authority with regard to his willingness and ability to work. The work sought is that which the individual considers suitable to his abilities. He is considered to be "actively seeking" work if he has made at least one bona fide application during the four week period prior to interview. This view of unemployment is in harmony with typical Western economic analysis. According to that analysis, goods and services (and the costs of producing them) are valued in terms of the preferences of the enormous number of individuals who make decisions about working, spending, and saving.

Unemployment As a Product of Modern Specialized Production

Perhaps a clear majority of the world's population live in subsistence economies, whose inhabitants cannot even imagine what is meant by

3

"unemployment." The Wotinsky's estimated their numbers at 57 percent of the world's population in 1948—8.5 percent of the people of the Americas, 94 percent of the Asians, 73 percent of the Africans, and 25 percent of those in Oceania.[1]

Unemployment of the type that disturbs modern economies is unknown in subsistence economies. Primitive tongues have no word for the concept. Periods of hard work alternate with leisure that sometimes comes in tiring and boring excess. But excess of leisure is not unemployment because additional work is not sought.

Poverty is also the lot of those in subsistence economies—if one measures their standard of living against even the poorest county in the United States. An outside observer might hesitate to describe those living in subsistence economies as "fully" employed, but he might say that they have achieved some kind of bliss point where work effort is in optimal balance with the fruits of labor. In this respect their social systems outshine the world's modern economies.

What is it that makes the idea of unemployment foreign to dwellers in primitive societies? No unemployment exists, I think, because their societies are small enough, their alternatives few enough, and their range of preferences visible enough to each other as to place the economic side of their social lives within a directly comprehensible administrative frame. It is possible to see what can be done. It is not too hard to come to an understanding about how much is worth doing. Means exist to induce each person to make an appropriate contribution and there are ways to see that each gets a share of output according to his needs. As a result there is little or no gap between group and individual aspirations to have more, and no great difficulties in finding work in order to get the added production when it is desired.

The subsistence society does not thrust upon its members the vast and prickly "information problem" that modern man must handle more or less continuously from youth at least until retirement. The member of a subsistence economy need not consider that his source of livelihood may be lost because of new developments in other regions. He need not forecast and adjust to technological developments, shifts of consumer tastes, or new discoveries of raw materials. As a result he will not find himself asking if he should seek another job, undertake retraining, or quit work to try another region. Much of the year the member of a subsistence economy may have little to do, but alternatives are few inside of his limited horizon. He has a place and is not impelled to look for another one. Part of the reason may be lack of vision of attainable goals, but more fundamentally it is because an optimal adjustment has been attained between economic ends and means.

All is quite different in modern specialized society. Discovery of what an individual, and society in general, can do and needs to do requires intelligence, trial and error, and some luck. Those who undertake to organize enterprises must cover heavy costs and take risks in order to explore both product and factor markets. Modern workers must seek a place in a poorly understood, constantly changing, economy. To gain social approval, the worker must make himself attractive enough to some employer, public or private, to win a job; must maintain performance subject to loss of position, income and social acceptance; and must at times be judged against the cold standard of efficiency relative to other people, other techniques, and other regions. He can lose a job, he can fail to find another one promptly. In short, he can be unemployed and resent it, even while eating well.

Little wonder that the social contribution of work becomes unduly subordinate to the value of the job as a source of personal income, that the individual joins with others to form organizations designed to claim control over as many jobs as possible so as to distribute them among its members, that our nation, whose minimum wage yields a full-time annual income well above the average family income in the world, transferred about 14.5 percent of total consumption expenditures via social insurance, health, and public aid programs in 1969, plus another 7.5 percent for education.

Increasingly there is acceptance of the idea that such large transfers should be able to underwrite for each person a *legal right* to some minimum level of income whether or not he is disposed to make any contribution to his society by way of productive effort.

Some see the individual as needlessly alienated from his society by the lack of such support combined with the difficulty of finding stable employment. The individual is seen as confused and frustrated because he does not know how to be useful to others and so fulfill himself.

The Social Costs of Unemployment Are
Not Fully Accounted for in
Modern Labor Markets

An unemployed person remains a consumer. He consumes some of the output produced by those currently at work, aided, perhaps, by capital equipment paid for by his past savings. His consumption is a cost borne by others which they escape once he becomes employed again. Nevertheless, the job-seeker is sympathized with and supported by the community.

Most people feel that there is a scarcity of jobs. Moreover, our innovative, dynamic economy requires constant shifting of working age people from firm to firm, industry to industry, and region to region. These shifts are beneficial overall, but are costly and painful to many of the individuals affected by layoffs. In addition, many, quite properly, do not seek employment. It is agreed that the handicapped, the disabled, those weakened by age or carrying special responsibilities should be supported by others.[a]

---

[a] It is necessary to emphasize the legitimacy of a decision not to work. The decision to work at all, like the decision to work more than some particular number of hours per year with some particular degree of intensity, is a decision that ideally will balance the cost of additional work against all the gains from work. Costs are high for the

In general a person will not be allowed to fall below some minimum standard of living whether or not he works. Nevertheless, a person who does not produce things of value imposes certain costs upon those who do. While those at work may be quite willing to carry those costs, the costs should not be left out of account, as they are at present, when decisions to work and to hire are being made. The costs are considerable.

Because the costs borne by others do not appear in the labor market, an employer must pay the full wage of an employee in spite of the fact that by hiring the person he relieves others in society of the cost of supporting the unemployed person. Looked at from another vantage point, the employer pays the full cost of the employee, but the employee's position is bettered only by the difference between what he then earns and what he would have received had he remained unemployed. It is not surprising, therefore, that unemployment, and the relative underuse of labor, continues and constantly threatens to worsen as specialization and affluence advance.

And now the thesis: *Every person can be made better off if the costs of providing income security can be reorganized, mobilized, and utilized to improve the effectiveness of the labor markets.*

American Experience

The remainder of this chapter presents the more significant trends in output per capita, welfare expenditures and inflation, and briefly examines the policies that are related to them. We find that real output per capita has grown faster than expected, and that the basic conditions surrounding opportunities to work seem to have improved. Affluence has not reduced unemployment, overcome inflation, or reduced the demand for welfare payments. On the contrary, rising affluence seems to have stimulated a great expansion of welfare.

Policies adopted to expand employment opportunities just after World War II have not reduced unemployment to generally acceptable levels but have produced inflation. Preliminary reasons are advanced to indicate why we should not expect better results from these policies in the future, and why wage and price controls can not reasonably be expected to improve matters.

The information presented in this chapter is intended to prepare the reader to look at the interconnections between welfare programs, unemployment and inflation in a new way and so to be more receptive to a different set of policies based upon the analysis of these interrelated aspects of modern life.

---

disabled, and the gains to himself and others may be small. Likewise, the gain from intensive and prolonged job search by a highly productive person to find a job where his specialized abilities are fully used may offset the loss of output he could have contributed from lesser jobs he could have taken during a long period of search. This matter is refined and examined intensively in the following chapters.

Growth of Affluence, Effect on Unemployment and Participation Rates

Scarcely anyone in the boom year 1929 would have believed that forty years later real income per capita would have doubled. Yet per capita real income has more than doubled. Actually, real *consumption* per capita has doubled. That is to say, if one subtracts from total income everything that business spends for investment and everything spent by government for goods and services (which includes the military, highways and education), leaving only consumption, and if one then adjusts that figure downward to allow for price changes, and adjusts it downward once again to take full account of the increase in population, there is still a doubling in forty years.

In 1929, prior to the stock market crash, it was commonly believed that a new era of perpetual prosperity had been inaugurated. Stalin's hope was not to surpass, but only to come close to matching the performance of such companies as the Ford Motor Company. America, with a social security program limited largely to workman's compensation and a few laws protecting women and children, was regarded as a worker's paradise.

Joseph A. Schumpeter put it this way in his 1942 edition of *Capitalism, Socialism and Democracy*: "Now if the system had another run such as it had in the sixty years preceding 1928 and really reached the $1,300 *per head of population* [i.e., double the 1928 level of per capita real income in 50 years] it is easy to see that all of the desiderata that have so far been espoused by any social reformers—practically without exception, including even the greater part of the cranks—would either be filled automatically or could be fulfilled *without significant interference with the capitalist process*."[2]

This income goal has been achieved a decade sooner than Schumpeter's optimistic extrapolation, and for a population 27 percent larger than his estimate. This in spite of heavy diversion of resources to military purposes (up from 1.6 to 12.6 percent of consumption), heavy profits taxes, heavy progressive income taxes, and much regulation, all of which Schumpeter viewed as interferences that sap the vigor of capitalist processes.

The chronically persistent fears of those who feel that "the system" must run into a dead end have not only failed to materialize, but expansion has accelerated. Neither the closing of the frontier, the dramatic reduction of agriculture's manpower needs to less than 5 percent of the labor force, the population explosion, the always asserted imminent exhaustion of resources, nor automation and cybernation—none of these, singly or in combination —have reversed the growth of income per capita. Nor have they limited employment opportunity. The facts are that the labor force is a *larger* percentage of the population over sixteen, and that the unemployment rate of this expanded labor force is, if anything, lower than in the 1920s despite a declining number of farmers who are not subject to unemployment.[b]

---

[b] The overall data obscure important shifts. Thus the percentage of the population in the labor force (the "participation rate") grew although the percentage of the men of college age in the labor force, as typified by the eighteen-to-nineteen-year-old group,

The overall data are shown in figure 1–1.

These are surprising truths. It is reasonable to suppose a priori that when people have higher incomes fewer will seek work, and that those who seek work will be more choosy, thus taking a longer time between jobs. The first expectation, if realized, would lower the percentage in the labor force, and the second would raise the unemployment rate. Together they would reduce the rate of growth. These expectations seem all the more reasonable because it has become easy to get unemployment compensation to cover part of living costs between jobs, because proportionately so many more youth now stay out of the labor force while they complete high school and attend college, and because proportionately so many more older people can choose to retire. The relatively low unemployment rates in recent years are also surprising when one reflects that a much larger percentage of the labor force was once self-employed farmers who could scarcely be unemployed. Finally, it is surprising that unemployment rates are not higher when it is realized that the dynamic growth of our economy more than ever requires shifting from job to job and area to area.

The higher participation rate in the labor force and continued moderate unemployment rate is due to little-noticed but important long-run changes.

Employability has been greatly enhanced by the improved versatility of the labor force due to higher educational attainment, the lowering or dropping of discriminatory barriers which limited the opportunities of women and minority races, and the greatly increased mobility of the population due to the private car, the rented trailer and truck, and the rising demand for housing that has permitted moves with less risk of loss on the sale of one's home. Rapid, low-cost air transportation and cheap, long distance telephone rates also tend to expand the labor markets and improve the prospects of job-seekers.

Still, it is somewhat surprising that these influences should have predominated over the already mentioned influences making for smaller participation rates and greater unemployment.

Some readers may believe that these improvements are counterbalanced by a worsening distribution of income. The statistical evidence gives superficial support to their position. The difference between the number of dollars earned by the top and the bottom fifths of income earners is substantially greater today than in the past. Thus the average income of the families in the lowest fifth in 1935–6 was $337, while the average income of the highest fifth was $4,216, a difference of $3,879. For 1962 the comparable figures are $1,662 and $16,505 for a difference of $14,843.[3] It would appear that the gap between the rich and the poor had more than tripled.

Part of the difference is simply inflation. Still, if incomes are corrected for price changes (using 1950-value dollars) the difference is $6,984 in

---

fell from 80.5 to 69.6 percent between 1947 and 1969. The labor force also lost many men over sixty-four years of age, the percentage of those in the labor force dropping off from 47.8 to 27.2 percent. These declines were offset almost entirely by the higher participation rates of women of prime labor force age.

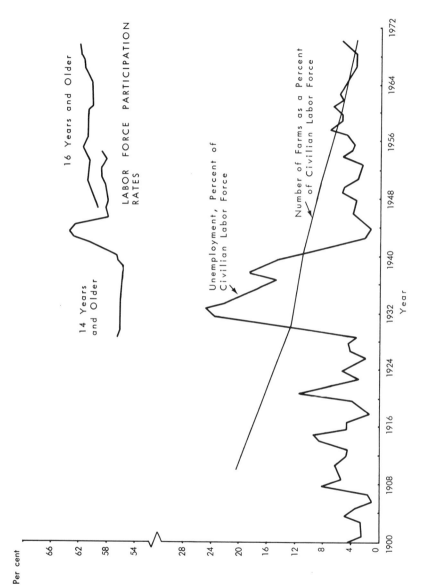

Figure 1-1. Labor Force Trends.

1935–36 and $11,903 in 1962. But even this is quite misleading. The lower fifth increased their share of total family income from 4.1 to 4.6 percent, while the upper fifth found its share reduced from 51.7 to 45.5 percent of family income. The upper 5 percent of families dropped from 26.5 to 19.6 percent of total family income although their average income rose from $15,582 to $22,840 1950-value dollars, an increase much larger in absolute terms than the whole family income of the average family in the lowest fifth.

Absolute differences have become greater, but relative differences smaller. Stated in terms of rates of growth, the poor's *share* of national income is increasing more rapidly than the share of the rich. The relative shares, which reflect the dynamic processes at work in the economy, are the more relevant ones because rates of change tell more about future income distribution.

There are other reasons why relative changes should be given more attention than absolute differences in income between income groups. Most important among them is a gross bias that exists because they are reporting incomes for a single year. The lowest fifth of income earners include a disproportionate number of very young individuals just getting started, or still supporting themselves while working their way through college, businessmen who suffered losses in that year (and may have large *negative* incomes) but who have assets enough so as to suffer no privation, and others with temporarily low incomes. Likewise, the highest fifth will include many with exceptional "windfall" incomes that may never be repeated, along with others such as professional sports figures and actors who may have very high incomes for only a very few of the many years of their lives. There are no satisfactory data which describe the degree of inequality of lifetime earnings to my knowledge, but it is certainly very much more equal than the distribution shown here. One wonders what the share of the lowest fifth, highest fifth, etc. would be in any given year if lifetime earnings were identical for all.

In any case, the trend towards more equal family incomes continues as shown in figure 1–2. Recent data taken from the *Statistical Abstract* differ somewhat from those for earlier periods taken from *Historical Statistics*, so both figures are given for overlapping years.

The data show the share of national income going to the upper 5 percent of families to have been virtually cut in two since 1929. A large part of this represents a declining share of the highest 1 percent of income receivers. Families in the lowest fifth improved their share by about 1.6 percent of national income, an increase of nearly 40 percent. The lowest 40 percent of families increased their share more than 44 percent. These data show a marked movement toward equality of income distribution.

The movement toward income equality is entirely in conformity with expectations because virtually universal education through high school plus cheap college education in publicly-supported institutions and greatly

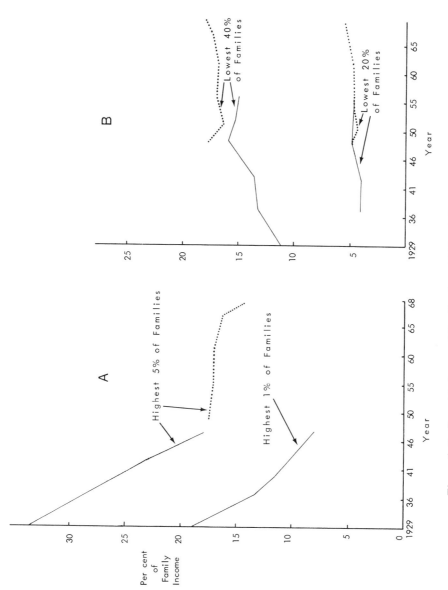

Figure 1-2. Trend in Income Distribution: 1929-68 (Two data Sources).

improved financial institutions must be expected to make economic opportunity more nearly equal.

The reader may be interested to know that the highest family income in the lowest fifth of families was $3,289 in 1968. A family receiving $16,200 was in the highest 10 percent in that year. These are $3900 and $19,100 in January 1972 prices.

Growth of Welfare Programs:
A Welfare "Crisis"

Everyone in 1929 would have thought a pollster crazy or joking had he included the possibility of a demand for transfers to the poor so great as to be called a "welfare crisis" in a prospective situation where real per capita income was doubled, more people were at work, the unemployment situation was no worse, and the distribution of income had become more equal than in 1929. Schumpeter, writing from the perspective of 1942, would have agreed. He wrote, "One way of expressing our result is that, if capitalism repeated its past performance for another half century starting in 1928, this would do away with anything that according to present standards could be called poverty, even in the lowest strata, pathological cases alone excepted."[4] Schumpeter was wise enough to foresee a substantial need for welfare payments, but he believed that they would be a light burden, certainly no "crisis," unless mismanaged.

Figure 1–3 gives an impression of the long term growth of health, education, and welfare expenditures. In 1929 per capita expenditures for welfare was $70, 1969-value dollars, 71 percent of which went to education. In 1969 publicly financed welfare costs were $616 per capita, only 34 percent of which went to education. Put another way, public expenditures for health, education, and welfare rose from 4.1 percent to 14.1 percent of Gross National Product. In 1969 health, education, and welfare expenditures amounted to 21.9 percent of consumption expenditures.

The belief that a crisis exists is not so much related to the size or to the growth of welfare expenditures as it is to the belief that the enormous expenditures are not producing desirable results. Poverty persists, fears rise that a generation is coming of age that does not wish to support itself, and there is the shocking revelation that less than half of the poor receive any aid.[5]

Robert J. Lampman has estimated that about 57 percent of 1967 social welfare expenditures under public funds (exclusive of education) are transfers to those defined as poor prior to the transfer.[6]

If this percentage holds for 1969, about 8.2 percent of total expenditures for consumption purposes were transfers to those families classified as poor in that year. Still, 4.8 million families and 4 million unrelated individuals remained in the "poor" category.

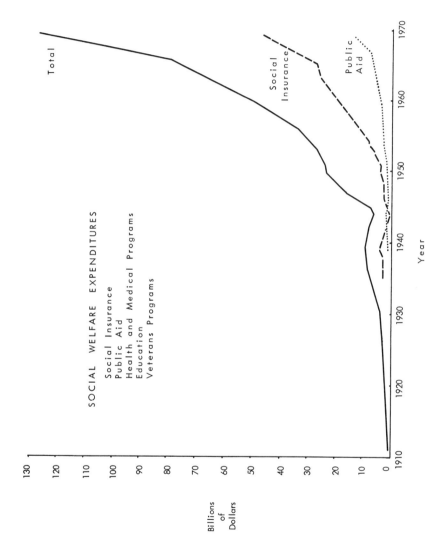

Figure 1-3. Social Welfare Expenditures.

Growth of Welfare Programs
since World War II

It is interesting to compare the growth of social security programs during the generally prosperous postwar decades with that during the Great Depression of the 1930s. The basic data are shown in the two panels of figure 1–4. The 1930s saw the introduction of Old Age and Survivors Insurance (OASI) and crash programs of work relief and expanded public assistance. Education took 2 to 3 percent of Gross National Product throughout the period, but expenditures for welfare and health rose from 1.5 to about 8 percent of GNP during the depression. These expenditures fell off rapidly as a percent of GNP as full employment was regained in 1941.

The forecast postwar "reconversion depression" which was widely expected to drive unemployment rates up to at least 8 percent after the war did not come to pass despite the precipitous dismantling of the American armed forces prior to the awareness of the cold war and the Korean invasion. Manpower was absorbed in civilian production as wartime price, wage and other controls were removed. GNP rose to unprecedented heights that reduced the still substantial expenditures on education, health, and welfare to approximately the same percentage of GNP that had existed in 1929. But the share to welfare and health remained at about two-thirds, with only one-third going to education. In 1945 an expanded education budget took only 1.5 percent, and the total health, education and welfare budget only 4.5 percent of GNP.

One might have thought that the return to low levels of unemployment after the war would be accompanied by continued low levels of welfare expenditures.

The lower panel of figure 1–4 shows how much more rapidly health, education, and welfare expenditures have grown as compared to the overall growth of output. (A horizontal line would indicate a growth rate equal to the growth of total output.) Educational expenditures have grown more rapidly than GNP, as would be expected because of the "baby boom." But publicly financed expenditures for health, social insurance, and public aid grew far more rapidly than expenditures for education. These expenditures, which we shall refer to as "welfare," grew faster than output in a time of low unemployment and rising per capita income. Indeed it was, and continues to be, the most rapidly expanding major activity in the nation.

Inflation-Deflation since 1920

It is common knowledge that when prices are stable or falling, unemployment is "too high." Leading economists agree. See, for example, James Tobin's presidential address to the American Economic Association, "Inflation and Unemployment."[7] But it has not always been so. Prices fell during the great peacetime prosperity in the late 1920s, and that is not an isolated instance in American history.

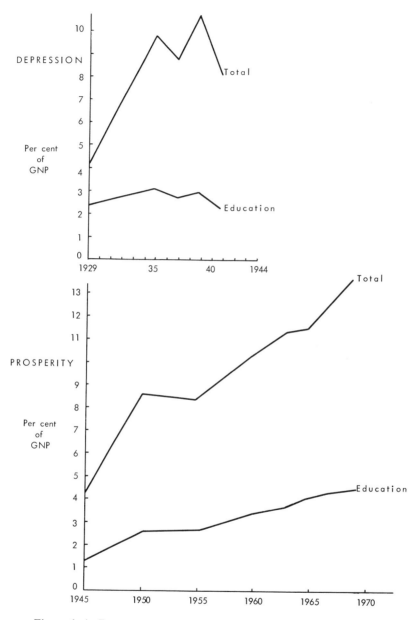

Figure 1–4. Response to Depression and Response to Prosperity.

Government policies with regard to unemployment changed drastically during the Great Depression. Even before President Franklin Roosevelt's New Deal, President Hoover signed a price support bill for agriculture, instituted the Reconstruction Finance Corporation to assist enterprises threatened by failure, and agreed to the Norris-LaGuardia Act that removed serious obstacles confronting labor unions. The Republican failure to stem rising levels of unemployment was made the prime campaign issue for the elections of 1932, 1936 and established a new responsibility of federal government. This was formalized in the Full Employment Act of 1948 which established a Council of Economic Advisors, and a Joint Committee of Congress to study economic affairs. In a sense the act was ratified when President Eisenhower, a Republican, made no effort to change it upon his election, but rather strengthened the position of the Council of Economic Advisors in his administration.

The experimentation with fiscal policy, which began willy-nilly in the Hoover administration and was thought contrary to "sound economies" by many, found economic rationale in J. M. Keynes' incredibly influential *The General Theory of Employment, Interest and Money* and became firmly institutionalized in the Eisenhower administration. We will argue that the close association of rising prices with low levels of unemployment began with these events. Persistent inflation during prosperity dates from the time that government intervened in markets and undertook conscious use of monetary and fiscal policy to expand the money demand for goods and services in order to assure full employment.

Theories and Policies

As already stated, the principal purpose of this book is to advance a different theory of unemployment. The key element is that in modern economies important gains are lost that would accrue to many presently employed people if more people were employed doing something of net value. These gains cannot, under present circumstances, be given any weight by either prospective employees or their employers when they make their decisions. The proposed theory can, perhaps, be better understood if the alternative theories which are now in vogue, and the policies based upon them, are summarized.

Alternative Theories: Monetary
and Fiscal Policy

The standard theory and government policies relating to full employment during the last thirty years is called the "new economics" of Keynes. Reasons are given in chapter 4 and its appendix for believing that the promise offered by this body of theory has been exhausted. Several comments can be made in a preliminary way at this point. When unemployment above some acceptable level appears, the new economics calls for an expansionist fiscal and cooperating monetary policy which acts by means of some combination of tax cuts, spending programs, or other devices facilitated by appropriate actions of the Federal Reserve System to stimulate consumer demand, private investment, and/or government programs.

Expanded welfare expenditure has been a favorite channel for increased government expenditure. But price and wage levels have risen before the targeted full employment level has been reached. This has been a matter of chronic concern, with the rate of inflation seen as an unfortunate constraint upon the elimination of excess unemployment.[8]

One important difficulty is that no objective, logically tight, definition of full employment has been formulated.[9] As a practical matter, an *ad hoc* working definition has been accepted as the goal for policy purposes. Inflationary tendencies, mobility and information problems make 4 to 6 percent unemployment the working definition. Increasingly, even 4 percent is decried as unacceptably high. The record suggests that if 5 to 6 percent unemployment were accepted, monetary and fiscal intervention would not have longer run inflationary effects and so would "work." But an attempt to reduce unemployment to the 2 to 4 percent range by monetary and fiscal means seems certain to produce inflation while leaving unemployment ultimately still in the 4 to 6 percent range once people adjust their expectations to the rising price and wage levels.[10]

Alternative Theories: Wage and Price Controls

Modern nations sometimes attempt to push the unemployment rate down to 4 percent or less without causing inflation by using its policy power through gentle threats to be reasonable in wage and price decisions, or by imposing outright wage and price controls. These policies have strong superficial appeal, because it seems obvious that the expanding money demand for goods and services that monetary and fiscal policy ensures must then go to increased employment and output rather than to mere wage and price inflation.

The results of such policies have been disappointing, both here and abroad. I think it is because they do nothing to bring the individual's costs of hiring additional workers into line with their social costs. At this point, however, consider only the practical side of this problem for Western nations and for the Soviet Union.

In the West, controls have had limited successes during short wars, such as World War II. But consider the special conditions that prevail during short wars: (1) there is a well-defined national purpose—win the war; (2) there is widespread confidence that the administration knows best and is operating in the best interests of the nation as a whole—it is *the* recognized expert; (3) nearly everyone has close relatives who are facing death in their defense, and whose support requires the rather small sacrifices involved in not trying to get a wage increase, or not dealing on a black market—the sacrifices are seen as small relative to those that others must bear; and (4) there is widespread confidence that the sacrifices demanded are temporary—the war will soon be over.

None of these conditions prevails under peacetime conditions. Moreover, during the war people invariably accumulate reserves of money and credit that create serious inflationary pressures after the war.

If peacetime wage and price controls are to work, they must make sense. Emotional patriotism will not sustain them for long. And they must not build up large savings in the hands of individuals that will enable them to live without working in just a few years.[c]

The real trouble with the controls is that, however sensible they may seem as abstractions, they never make sense to those who must live with them. There is also an insidious aspect of controls. In each specific case where they do not make sense it always seems that matters can be improved by a little, rather obvious, additional regulation. But the consequences of additional regulation, when attempted, always include unforeseen and undesired side effects. The undesired consequences make a little, perhaps quite a little, additional regulation seem not so much wise as really necessary and inevitable. Eventually the multiplication of regulations leads to such great inefficiency and dissatisfaction that "bold, innovative decentralization" of the sort now being tried in some Communist nations becomes popular. In the meantime, inflation continues under controls and unemployment has, at the very best, been concealed in inefficiency. Modern economies are too complex for any simple set of rules, and 10,000 pages of explanations and exceptions do not help matters.

Alternative Theories: Central Planning

Centrally planned economies apparently have the same problem despite virtually complete control systems which go far beyond wage and price controls. Consider the Soviet system.

It is important to realize that the Soviet economy is very much simpler than the U.S. economy, although its complexity has grown rapidly as it has become more productive. The reader should know that no method is known whereby a nation can become more productive without becoming more specialized and thus more complex. Specialization involves information, mobility, and related conditions that seem to lie at the heart of the modern welfare, employment, and inflation dilemmas.

The Russian academician, A. Dorodnitsyn, whose *Izvestia* article of May 15, 1963 is reported by Leon Smolinski and Peter C. Wiles, estimates that the Soviet's planning task of the early 1960s was 1,600 times more complex than the task for the simpler 1928 economy.[11] The Russian mathematician, Glushkov, vice-president of the Ukrainian Academy of

---

[c] With no excess saving there will be no need for any controls to eliminate inflationary pressures.

Science (*Literaturniia gazeta*, Sept. 25, 1962), also reported by Smolinski and Wiles, writes that under the existing conditions the volume of planning tends to increase by at least the square of the output. Thus he predicted a 36-fold increase in the planning effort by 1980, an increase which, if realized, would, he says, *require the whole adult manpower of the Soviet Union*, leaving no one to carry out the planned production, if the planning techniques used in 1962 were still relied upon in 1980.

It is appropriate to note that the American economy of 1960 already produced a much greater variety of products, and had a much more specialized labor force than the one envisioned by Gloshkov for the Soviet economy in 1980. No one, least of all the Russian academicians, believes that the Soviet information and planning system comes at all close to matching the efficiency of the American system, where much less manpower is devoted to management, and output per man is approximately three times as high.

It is commonly believed, however, that the Soviet system at least achieves full employment, and some believe that this achievement compensates adequately for production inefficiencies. On the face of it, it would seem that even very inefficient planning should virtually eliminate unemployment. Output is not bound by the need of the enterprises to make profits. Hence firms can maintain the demand for labor in the face of losses, and recover funds to pay for its resources, if need be, from government-owned banks, or from the state budget. Likewise, population can be held in present employment, often in agriculture, where they can find *something* to do, while urban enterprises and housing are prepared for them. This should avoid the possibility of a premature flow of manpower to the cities, manpower drawn by rumors and false hopes and often stranded without jobs and without the means to return home. Yet thirty-five years of intensive planning effort which utilizes all these devices apparently does not suffice.

An "unpublished" speech attributed to the Soviet economist, A. G. Aganbegian, appeared in the Italian-language weekly, *Bandiera Rossa* (Red Banner), Rome, July, 1956, and was translated and published in *Joint Publications Research Service*, no. 220, September 1, 1965. This speech is so highly critical of the Soviet information and planning system as to merit classification as an impassioned attack. Yet many statistics are given which are basically in conformity with known conditions. The writer asserts that Russian industrial capacity is only 70 percent utilized, that in large cities 8 percent of the population able to work are unable to find work, and that the percentage not able to find work rises to between 25 to 30 in smaller and medium-sized cities. He says that this is so in the face of a commitment of 30 to 40 million of the 100 million workers to defense (a high figure as compared to other estimates), and a system that holds large redundant manpower reserves in agriculture where people earn a net income of only 1.5 rubles per day from collective labor plus another 3.5 rubles from their private plots. He asserts that if the people were allowed to leave the countryside, hardly anyone would remain behind, despite, one must suppose, the employment situation in the cities.

A. G. Aganbegian, if he is the true author, lays the blame for all of this, and much more that is passed over here, primarily upon mistaken commitment of resources (toward heavy industry), the system of planning, incentives and management which does not correspond to real requirements, and "an absolute lack of information" compounded of secrecies, inaccuracies and lies.

Aganbegian may overstate the problems, but there can be no doubt that a nation with a severe continental northern climate will have highly seasonal production of agricultural products and many services, such as transportation, as well as some industrial production, such as outdoor construction. As a progressive nation, superior processes will displace obsolete ones, obsoleting the skills of some workers and forcing them to seek other work. Then too, even in the days of labor books and attempted job freezes, the labor turnover rate in Russian industry was twice that of the United States. Many must still quit their jobs to seek another. So despite three years of compulsory military service in Russia, which occupies the ages of greatest job shifting by American youths, substantial unemployment must exist in the U.S.S.R. (We exclude from consideration those officially excluded from the opportunity to work as a penalty for economic or political offenses.) These reasons for unemployment are the same as for all other dynamic industrial economies: seasonal changes of demand, dynamic shifts required by technological progress, and voluntary shifts to attempt to better oneself.

Nevertheless, an unemployment rate of 8 percent or more seems extraordinarily high. Two alternative explanations may be added to those given in *Baniera Rossa*. Costs of capital to Russian firms are artificially low, and labor is therefore relatively expensive. While this would result in an underuse of labor if the firms were profit-maximizers, it is not likely to affect Russian firms' demands for labor. Russian managers are motivated more intensely to meeting or surpassing output goals and less intensely toward maximizing profits. Therefore each will use all of the resources he can muster to meet or surpass the output goal.

Aganbegian probably has a concept of "unemployment" quite different from that used in the United States. His probably is not based on the subjective preferences of individuals. Many of those he calls "unemployed" are probably people who do not wish to work for one reason or another and are not in the labor force by U.S. definition. Wives who do not feel the need to work at all—in spite of the free nursery schools and great official pressure which attempts to drive all married women into the "liberated" and "nondiscriminatory" labor markets—would be "able to work." But they would not be working by Aganbegian's standards (if he accepts the official view) and so would be classified as "unemployed." But others truly are not working because they cannot find work they like. In the Russian economy overemployment, in the sense of socially coerced employment, exists simultaneously with unemployment.

Neither overemployment nor unemployment is optimal. Neither centrally planned nor free enterprise economies attain optimal levels of employment.

2

Basis for Theory of Unemployment: Analysis of Preferences and Income Opportunities

Some rather formal tools of analysis are needed to provide a basis for logically tight definitions of "labor force" and "unemployment," to gain understanding of existing and proposed welfare programs, and to grasp the possibilities that they offer for modifications that can reduce unemployment and inflationary pressures to the vanishing point.

Formal analysis can be stated in mathematical formulae, graphs, and words. Only words and graphs are used here, however. A reading of the words alone may suffice, but the time taken to understand the graphs gives added clarity and power.

Basically, the analysis requires a careful juxtaposition of the preferences of individuals against their income opportunities. The income conditions are objective and can be altered by governmental decisions to tax and/or subsidize individuals. Preferences are subjective and cannot be measured directly or manipulated with any precision by government actions. Preferences must be inferred from behavior. Our principal objective in this chapter is to discover the shape of the preference functions that can be inferred from recorded actions of individuals under differing circumstances.

The division between preferences and income opportunities may seem arbitrary to the reader because the expressed preferences of individuals depend in large part upon the incomes and work opportunities that they face. But it is not arbitrary because preferences include undeveloped preferences relevant to all levels of income, wage rates, and prices of goods. Preferences refer to a complete preference function with an indefinitely large number of dimensions.

Common sense informs us that one's preference function contains a highly diverse congeries of interrelationships and conditions which varies over one's lifetime and differs greatly between individuals. Common sense informs us, in a word, that scientific analysis of preferences is a hopeless task. But common sense is often incorrect. It tells us that the world is flat and that a chunk of steel is not composed mostly of empty space within which billions of particles spin at tremendous speeds.

Progress in the analysis of preferences is by no means as advanced as the study of atomic particles, but even the simple analysis presented here provides a much better basis for social engineering than does the usual moralistic notions of what people *should* do, and repressive impulses to *make* them do what they should if they are to avoid prosecution under the law. The latter "political" kind of thinking has led the people of the world to form contentious and antagonistic groups, the negative aspects of which are beginning to overwhelm their historic virtues.

21

Analysis of preferences is possible because we are interested in the behavior of large groups of people so that individual idiosyncrasies average out. Analysis is facilitated because it is possible to group people together into rather homogeneous groups of known sizes so that they may be studied separately if there is reason to believe preferences differ. Then the total effect is estimated by combining the separate groups. It is possible to check our findings by comparing the results of our work with the findings of other investigators who have taken different approaches to the problem. Finally we can determine whether or not the implications of our analysis are consistent with well-established facts about labor markets.

The principal hypothesis we use is that many individual's preference functions as revealed by actual choices in differing circumstances tell us what others would do in those circumstances. It is reasonable to believe that the preference functions which are discovered in this way are stable because the patterns found for the various groups in different circumstances are quite consistent with each other. Consistency implies stability of the system of preferences because it follows from the assumption that the modal individual in every group changes his behavior when his income possibilities change so as to behave as others do who were already a member of the group he is joining. For example, a person whose health is impaired will tend to prefer part-time work, a woman whose children have grown up is more likely to desire full-time work; a family which has fallen heir to considerable income from property will tend to work fewer hours per year if nothing happens to increase their rate of pay from labor. For each case the behavior becomes similar to the characteristic behavior of people who already suffer poorer health, who are women with reduced family responsibility, or are families with greater wealth.

Major Groups of Workers

The largest single group of workers are males who work full time (35 hours a week or more) for 50 to 52 weeks a year. They comprised a little more than 40 percent of total labor force in 1968. An additional 16 percent of the workers were women who worked full time for 50 to 52 weeks per year. Together, these two groups accounted for about 75 percent of the total hours worked in 1968. About two-thirds of the remaining 25 percent of the work performed was done by full-time workers who worked less than 50 weeks a year. The remainder, less than 10 percent of the total, was performed by individuals working less than 35 hours a week and fewer than 50 weeks a year. At the other extreme, about 5 percent of all workers held two or more jobs.[1]

Each of the groups listed above can be subdivided according to their age, race, and other characteristics, but it may be unnecessary to do so. However, it would almost certainly be necessary if our object were to explain the participation rate (the proportion either working or seeking work), for it differs greatly by sex, race, and family responsibility. But it is not so evident that many subdivisions are necessary to account the behavior of either full-time or part-time workers. Those who have chosen to work full time obviously have the opportunity to do so and therefore a certain similarity of preferences must exist. It is reasonable to examine the variety of circumstances to which full-time workers have responded. They include wide differences of pay per hour, and income from sources other than labor during the current year. We will call this "non-work income." It may be that a single set of preferences (or "preference function") will turn out to be compatible with the many alternative opportunities. If so, it will give support to the thesis that the behavior of large groups of people is predictable from changes of the income opportunities which confront them. Only marginal, perhaps negligible, improvement of understanding would be forthcoming from costly efforts to disaggregate the data.

The same thing can be said for voluntary part-time workers, that is, those who desire part-time work. They account for about 85 percent of the part-time workers. In his circumstances, each voluntary part-time worker prefers to work part time. While the reason for prefering part-time work may differ greatly among individuals, the fact that it is preferred establishes an a priori presumption that significant similarities exist among the preferences for work, enjoyment of the things that work-income can buy, and leisure.

It will greatly simplify analysis if attention can be confined to these two groups which together account for 96 percent of the work done. So I proceed on this basis. The rest of this chapter develops the basic set of relationships used in later chapters, examines empirical data gathered by others in order to estimate the shape of the preference functions for full-time and part-time workers, and prepares the way for their application to matters of welfare, guaranteed minimum income, and unemployment.

Income Opportunities

Just about every income opportunity can be shown on a simple two-dimensional graph, such as figure 2–1. Suppose, for example, that a person will be able to consume an amount of goods and services worth $1,500 even if he does no work during some time period, say a year. This can be expressed by a single dot, point A, which shows his personal income of $1,500 as associated with zero hours of work. Alternatively, he might work full time for 50 weeks at $2 an hour, and thus earn $4,000. If he must work 2,000 hours before getting paid, as he may if he is a contractor, his opportunity is shown by the dot at point C. (Ignore the upward-sloping lines for the moment.) If he could keep the $1,500 from nonwork sources, his total income would then be $5,500. This is shown by point B, which shows an income of $5,500 associated with 2,000 hours of work. But if the individual loses the income from nonwork resources when he works, his income from working full time would again be only $4,000, as is shown by point C.

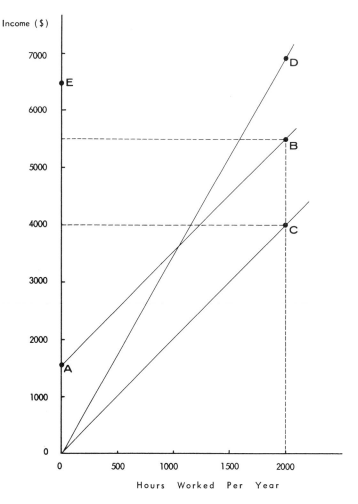

Figure 2-1. Some Income Opportunities.

Here are three income possibilities, or rather two pairs of income possibilities, A and B, and A and C. The choice that the individual makes between A and B, or A and C will tell us something about his preferences between working (and the things that he can get with the money earned) and leisure (the ability to organize his time to his liking, and to spend more time shopping so as to get the most out of his $1,500). If we know his preference structure we can answer such questions as whether or not he will work 2,000 hours to earn $4,000 more when he can have $1,500 without working; and, what is more interesting, whether or not he would work 2,000 hours to attain point B, when he would not work 2,000 hours to obtain point C, where he loses the $1500 when he works.

The detailed knowledge needed to predict what each individual would do does not exist. Some data about the behavior of some groups of individuals does exist which can be made to yield pretty good clues about what the normal work-leisure choices of groups of people are. The data themselves do not do much more than provide clues, but they are consistent with the expectations of long standing and very carefully thought out theories of consumer and worker behavior. Together, they are strong enough to give us useful insights into what is likely to happen when income possibilities are altered.

It should be clear that figure 2–1 can show the income opportunity for any amount of nonwork income and for any wage, however high, although the vertical axis must be extended upwards for annual incomes above $7,000. Thus the income from work for 2,000 hours of labor at $3.50 an hour is $7,000, and is shown by point D. The ability to receive $6,500 of nonwork income, as advocated by some, is shown by point E.

The effect of taxes on income can also be shown by plotting one point for the income before taxes, and another for the income after taxes, both at the same number of annual hours of work. The tax, of course, is the dollar amount designated by the vertical distance between such points.

Hours of Work

Most people seem to think that the hours of work are fixed at 40 per week, and that in most cases an employee must work 50 weeks a year. They do not think that the employee has much of any choice in the number of hours he will work a year. When that is the case, dots like A and B will describe all the choices that the individual has. He would have to choose between not working while receiving whatever low income he might receive, and working full time. His only remaining choice would be how hard to try to prepare himself in order to get a better job if he decided to work. He would have to decide whether or not it was worth the effort to try to attain the higher paying job and get to a point like D, or be content with the lesser job like C.

These are choices that each individual must make. But economists know that in fact there is also considerable variation in hours worked, especially when hours per year are considered, and especially when changes in income opportunities take effect over time. Thus they also think of the amount of work done as being a matter of decision by individuals. A student is likely to think that economists go to the other extreme and assume that the individual can work just the amount that he wants to. That is not quite true, but it is convenient to draw a nice straight line that shows *every* possible income that the person might receive at a given wage rate, depending upon the exact amount of time worked. Thus a worker whose wage is $2 an hour will earn $1,000 if he works 500 hours, $2,000 if he works 1,000 hours and so on. This "functional" relationship is shown by the line that starts at the origin (zero) and passes through point C. We will call such a line an *income opportunity line*.

Each person has at least one income opportunity line, and we follow the convention of calling the one that an individual is actually on "optimal." We disregard any others that he might have attained *except* those which will be presented to him if the government changes its welfare and tax programs. In those cases we will compare his present income opportunity line with the one that is offered in order to determine, if we can, the consequences of the policies for the amount of work that the person will wish to perform, and his income.

Three income opportunity lines are shown on figure 2–1. Besides OC, there is line AB and line OD. Line AB shows the individual's income possibility curve who has $1,500 of income from some nonwork source (investments, a pension, social security) and can also earn $2 an hour without having to give up any part of his nonwork income. Line OD shows all of the income possibilities for a person who has no nonwork income, but earns at the rate of $3.50 an hour. Another income possibility line could have been drawn in between A and C which would have shown the income possibilities for a person who will receive $1,500 if he does not work, but must pay the $1,500 back at the rate of 75¢ out of every $2 earned. Such a line is like the one that is proposed in many plans for a guaranteed minimum income, but the rate of recovery (the 75¢ per $2) is substantially lower that that called for by most plans.

Attempt to Infer the Preference Function for Low-Income, Full-Time Workers Working about Fifty Weeks a Year

The Income Opportunity Line

Admittedly this section attempts to conclude quite a lot from few data. Nevertheless, it is interesting in itself, broadly consistent with what has been discovered by costly and time consuming empirical studies, and tends to confirm the more carefully thought out applications of formal theory which attempt to explain the supply curve of labor by reference to the preferences of workers.

The data are those taken from the *U.S. Census Current Population Survey* by Christopher Green and Alfred Tella and analyzed in "Effect of Nonemployment Income and Wage Rates on the Work Incentives of the Poor," *The Review of Economics and Statistics,* November, 1969. They examined a sample of 2,000 families with low income (less than $7,000 a year), each of which received no income from welfare sources, was headed by a man between the ages of 25 and 60, and had at least one child living at home. Their data for 1965 are presented in table 2–1. The data for 1966 produce very similar relationships. The wage rates shown in table 2–1 and figure 2–2 are calculated from the midpoints of income classes except for Group A, where $1500 is used. This permits the use of these data to display the income possibility lines for each of the eight groups, which is done in figure

Table 2-1
Hours Worked and Income Received from Work and Nonwork Sources by
Low Income Families: 1965

Annual Income Class	Hours Worked		Average Nonwork Income	Wage Rate (calculated)	
	No nonwork income	With nonwork income		No nonwork income	With nonwork income
A. $ 0–2,000	1928	1729	$906	$0.78	$0.34
B. $2,000–2,999	2050	1875	773	1.22	1.00
C. $3,000–3,999	2120	1900	994	1.65	1.32
D. $4,000–6,999	2210	2125	550	2.48	2.38

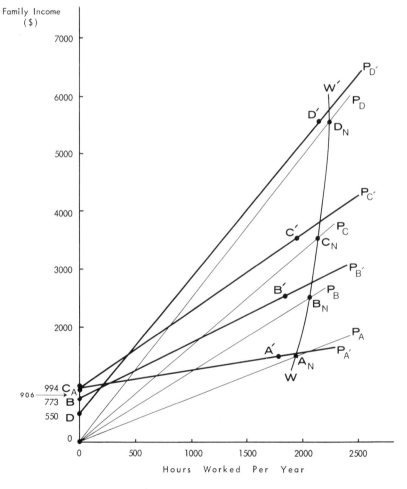

Figure 2–2. Income Possibility Lines for Low Six Groups of Income Families, 1965.

2–2. Thirteen heavy dots denote the actual data. Each dot is labeled with the capital letter that designates the income group to which it pertains. The four lines radiating from the origin (zero income and zero hours worked) and designated as P_A, P_B, P_C and P_D are relevant for families in the four income classes who have no income except from their own work. It is notable that those who enjoyed higher hourly earnings also worked longer hours as shown by line WW'. Most worked somewhat more than the conventional full time of fifty 40-hour weeks for 2,000 hours.

Some families with average annual incomes in each income group had some nonwork income, no part of which was from welfare. Presumably none of it had to be sacrificed if the person also secured income by working. The amount of nonwork income is shown by the appropriate letter on the vertical axis. Each family with nonwork income had the choice of attempting to live on that alone or working at a wage shown by the slope of their income opportunity line. For example, the B group (annual income of $2,000–$3,000) had nonwork income average $773 of nonwork income, and enjoyed the opportunity of earning about $1 an hour if it worked. These people actually worked only 1,875 hours during the year, as shown by point B', as compared to the 2,050 hours worked by families in the same income class who had no nonwork income. The latter's work effort and income is shown by point B_N. This reduction of 175 hours is consistent with the theoretical expectations developed below. It is easy to see that the same expectation is fulfilled for the other groups whose average annual incomes were alternatively $1,500, $3,500 or $5,000. This can be read from the "Hours Worked" column of table 2–1, or by comparing A' with A_N, C' with C_N, and D' with D_N. It is possible that some families faced by the same choice decided not to work. Green and Tella included in their study only the families that worked approximately full time.

The Implied Preference Function

The array of eight specific choices on the eight income possibility lines makes it possible to draw some inferences about the possible shapes of preference functions that can exist for people with different amounts of income and earning potential who choose to work full time.

It is best to begin by outlining the theoretical expectations about preference functions. The key concept used here is that of an "indifference curve." Six indifference curves are displayed in figure 2–3. The six drawn in are the ones that are consistent with the best adjustment possible for each of the six higher income classes shown in table 2–1 and figure 2–2. What is said applies to all indifference curves, but present discussion refers to curve I_B so that definite money values can be discussed.

An indifference curve gets its name from its central concept—the individual is entirely indifferent to any of the particular combinations of alternatives designated by a particular curve. One point, B_N, on indifference curve I_B is for an income of $2,500 in return for working 2,050 hours in a year.

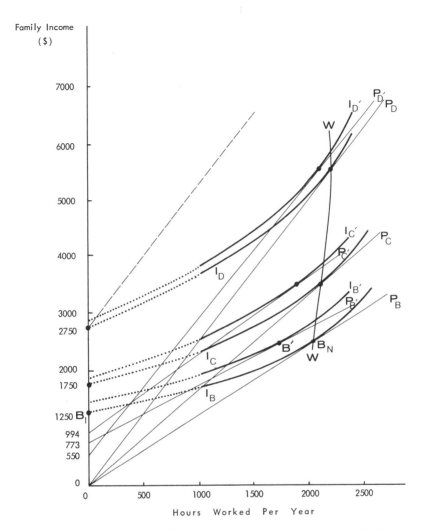

Figure 2–3. Income Possibility Line and Indifference Curves for Six Groups of Low Income Families, 1965.

If this is a true indifference curve the individual would not care at all whether he worked $2,050 hours for $2,500, or got $1,250 for no work. There are an indefinitely large number of alternative combinations of work and income just as satisfactory for him. Line I_B supposedly shows all such combinations.

We actually know only one preference point for each income possibility from Green and Tella's data, in this case that which connects 2,050 hours of work to an income of $2,500 when a person has no nonwork income and can earn a wage of $1.22. Technically, even that point is not on an indifference curve because it is drawn from the average behavior of a group of individuals, and not from any single individual. It would be more precise to refer to the "indifference curves" in figure 2–3 as "proximate group indifference curves," or to make up some new term to apply to them. It is probably less confusing, however, to use the term "indifference curve" loosely, as is often done, to refer to particular level of satisfaction that an individual within a group, or the group taken together, may achieve by attaining any of a number of different combinations of work and income.

The whole structure of indifference curves is called a *preference function*. The principal point to notice is that the more attractive combinations lie on the higher indifference curves. The easiest way to see this is to notice that the person will enjoy more income with the same amount of work at some point on a higher indifference curve. It follows that he is better off at every other point on the higher indifference curve, because each such combination of work and income is exactly as satisfactory to the individual as the one with that amount of work and the income associated with it. A corollary of the definition of an indifference curve is that no two of them may ever cross.

A simple application of indifference analysis is to show that people with some nonwork income are better off than the others who have the same total income. Consider the $2,000–3,000 income group in the Green and Tella data. There are two groups that have an average income of $2,500. Some earned the whole $2,500 from labor, but the others had $773 from savings, and so earned only $1,727 by labor during the year. It seems quite reasonable that the latter group should be considered better off, and indifference curves drawn in the conventional way will show that the second group is on the higher indifference curve, $I_{B'}$. Green and Tella find that among people who enjoy a given total income, those who get part of it from nonwork sources work fewer hours per year. This is what one would expect from theoretically-derived general shapes and relationships.

The shape of the individual curves is drawn on the basis of theoretical expectations which have been derived partly by thinking about the way people behave, and partly by looking at studies to see what their findings imply. We examine some of these studies later in the chapter and in chapter 3.

There are four strong reasons to believe that an individual's indifference curve will slope upward at an ever increasing rate as do the six curves shown in figure 2–3. First, it is clear that every hour of work subtracts an hour from leisure. Nearly everyone agrees that the less leisure one has the more an additional hour of leisure is worth to him. Second, the more things that one can buy with income, the more leisure it takes to enjoy those things. Third, one can get more value from a given income if one has more time for shopping. Fourth, it is probable that there is a rising disutility attached to additional hours of work, certainly beyond some minimum. For all of these reasons one must be compensated by increasing additions to income if he is to be as well off working a larger number of hours as when working a smaller number. The shape of curves like I_B simply describe this situation.

Their exact shape is not known, and in any case varies over time for any one individual, as well as from individual to individual.

If the indifference curves actually do have ever-increasing slopes, then one particular combination of work and income will be better than any other on a particular straight income opportunity line. If workers did what they preferred to do, the points shown by the six heavy black dots for positive amounts of work are points on their preference function. In that case their actual behavior will reveal a point on their indifference curve. We assume that here, and justify the assumption largely on the basis that markets behave as they would if individuals had preference functions of this type and were trying to attain the highest indifference curve that is within their reach.

Finding the correct steepness of the upward slope away from the point of tangency is a more difficult problem, and very little, if any, information exists about it. The curves in figure 2–3 are drawn on the assumption that a person with no nonwork income will be as content to live on half of his full time earnings if he can avoid working. The key curves are those where the person has no nonwork income—I_B, I_C, and I_D. Thus the person who can earn \$5,500 by working will decide whether or not to work by flipping a coin if he can get \$2,750 while idle. Note that he must give up the whole \$2,750 if he works. If he didn't have to give it up, his income opportunity line would be the dashed line rising from \$2,750, which immediately rises above indifference curve I_D.

The steepness of the slope of the indifference curves surely depends on such things as the health of the potential worker and his family responsibilities (or lack of them). The curves in figure 2–3 may be too steep, not steep enough or just right for the average behavior of the Green and Tella groups. They are drawn the way they are because workers such as furniture movers in their collective bargaining agreements agree to half pay if they are called to work but are released at once because no work is available. They are also roughly consistent with experimental studies, and with Green and Tella's own estimate of the expected reduction of hours worked as a result of a program to provide a guaranteed minimum income. Nevertheless, the slopes shown in Figure 2–3 should be considered as illustrative only. The more important analysis and conclusions are little affected by plausible differences in the steepness of the indifference curves.

Theoretical Studies

A long controversy about the shape of the supply of labor curve implies something about the shape of the indifference curves between work and money income. But the fact that a long controversy could exist suggests the truth that neither the theory nor the problems of measurement are nearly as simple as they seem to be at first glance. The difficulties are brought out clearly in an unpublished paper by Yoram Barzel and Richard McDonald, "The Supply Curve of Labor." They assume that the preference system (the whole range of indifference curves) is of a certain general mathematical form, which includes a particular set of sub-types referred to as a Cobb-Douglas utility function. This subtype is the one which Barzel and McDonald believe conforms best to a logically-deduced expectation, and it also agrees with the empirical evidence that they muster. The preference function inferred from the Green and Tella data does not quite fit the Cobb-Douglas pattern.

The most interesting characteristic of the Cobb-Douglas function for our present purposes is that what are termed "income" and "substitution" effects exactly offset each other when the wage rate available to a person is changed, provided that he has no income except that from wages. If the Green-Tella findings conformed exactly to the Cobb-Douglas form, the WW_1 line would have been exactly vertical. A person with such a preference system who became able to earn at a one-third higher wage rate would prefer to continue to work full time, and thus earn $6,000 rather than $4,000. The decision to work full time would be a compound of two elements. One is the income effect which denotes the fact that for any given amount of work effort he will have a higher income when his wages are increased. In our example he could have worked only two-thirds time and continued to earn $4,000 as before. Thus, other things being equal, we expect people to work somewhat less when their income rises because they can finance more enjoyable leisure time activities with less effort. But other things are not equal when the higher income is available only because of a higher wage rate. An additional hour of work adds more to income than before. If we look just at that fact, one would expect a person to be willing to work more hours because a given hour of work brings a greater return. This is the substitution effect. The income and substitution effects have opposite effects on the amount of work a person will wish to perform. As stated before, when a Cobb-Douglas utility function applies, these two influences exactly offset each other if the individual receives all of his income from wages.

Wealth and Income Effects

The amount that a person will wish to work is much affected by the source of his income. If he has income from nonwork sources such as inherited wealth, past savings and investments, a pension or social security payments, he will generally work less at any given wage rate. If he has debts to repay he will work more because his obligation to pay, whether he works or not, it can be thought of as a "negative nonwork income." The higher his wage rate, the less affected will be the amount of work that he will wish to perform because of nonwork income, or because of debt payments of a particular amount. All of this follows from the Cobb-Douglas utility function, such as that illustrated in figure 2–4.

Only two indifference curves are shown in figure 2–4. They are I_B and $I_{D'}$, taken from figure 2–3, but zero on the vertical scale is where minus $1,000 would be in figure 2–3. This adjustment brings the Green-Tella curves into

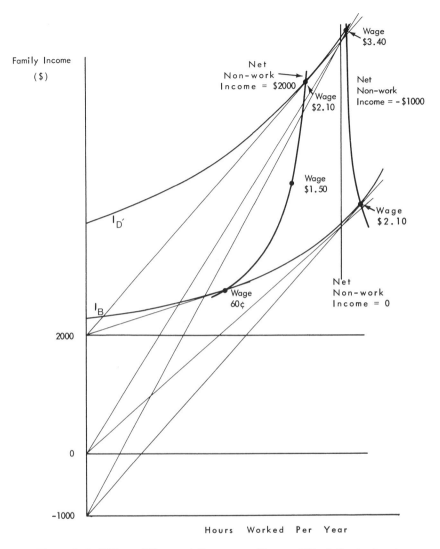

Figure 2–4. Effect of Nonwork Income on Hours of Work Desired under Cobb-Douglas Assumptions: Wages Variable.

approximate conformity with the Cobb-Douglas form. This can be interpreted as a failure of the Green-Tella data to conform exactly to the hypothesized mathematical preference function, or as a suggestion that the low income families had unreported nonwork economic resources. The resources could be nothing more than the knowledge that some support is available if their financial problems worsen. We assume that this is the case.

The preference function that yields a vertical supply of labor curve if all incomes come from wages (a higher wage showing up as a steeper slope of the line starting at zero on the vertical axis), also shows a desire to work more as wages rise when a person has some nonwork income ($2,000 in figure 2–4), and a desire to work fewer hours as wages rise if the person has debts (shown as *minus* $1,000 on figure 2 4) that must be paid whether or not he has income from wages. Note that at any given wage rate a person would work more if he has debts and less if he has nonwork income.

In this book we are particularly interested in the effects of social security payments, minimum income guarantees, and the like upon the performance of the economy. Such payments have the effect of giving a person some nonwork income under certain conditions. For example, in the state of Washington a family with a working member earning so little that it qualifies for public assistance will receive enough nonwork income (called a "benefit payment") to raise its income to a certain level which depends on the number of children and other characteristics. In effect, the benefit is reduced by 100 percent of the amount earned from work. From the standpoint of the family, the reduction of the benefit payment is a tax on the income from work. Its net income rises not at all because of its earnings from labor. In a very real sense, it is worse than that. If a member accepts a job that earns enough to take the family off welfare, but later loses the job, there can be a period of no income from any source during the time that it takes to regain qualification for renewed benefit payments. This important element of risk is not included in the analysis that follows.

The effects of benefit payments and benefit reductions associated with income from work are easily shown graphically. The effects could be predicted accurately if the preference functions of individuals were known. A reasonable expectation can be reached with the preference function developed earlier in the chapter. Consider figure 2–5. Two wage rates are shown, $1.65 and $3.00 per hour. In the absence of net nonwork income the same number of hours are worked at either wage rate. But as the benefit payment that an individual receives rises more and more above zero, an individual capable of earning a given wage, say $1.65, wishes to work less and less, even if he can keep the whole additional $1.65 for every hour worked. The line $B_{1.65}$ $B'_{1.65}$ shows the relationship for nonwork incomes between zero and about $2,800 a year.

These particular limits were chosen because they fit the Green and Tella data with the base line dropped $1,000 to make their data conform more closely to the Cobb-Douglas utility function. As it happens, the wage comes close to the official minimum wage of $1.60 for 1970–71, and the maximum benefit payment shown is not much greater than the $2,400 minimum family assistance payment that seems to be finding favor in Congress. At $2,400, the reduction of hours of work performed is about 25 percent. The reduction in the preferred amount of work by those able to earn higher wages is substantially less for any specific amount of benefit payment because it is a smaller part of their total income.

We will call the effect of nonwork income on the shape of the income opportunity line an "income from wealth effect" or "wealth effect" for convenience. This term is chosen because a benefit payment gives a person a

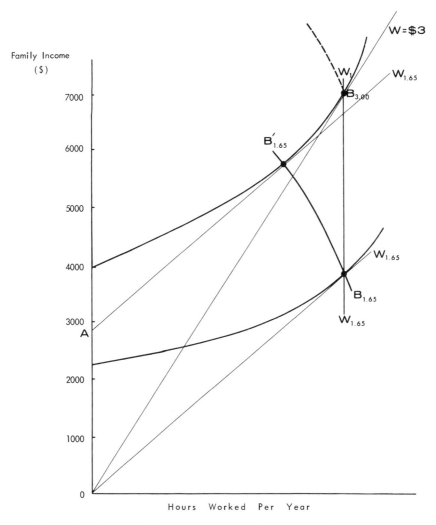

Figure 2-5. Predicted Response to Benefit Payments at Constant Wage Rates.

nonwork income that is closely analogous to income from personal wealth. Like income from personal wealth, it rests upon a governmental basis. Personal wealth exists because of the governmentally defined, regulated, protected and enforced institution of private property, and is certain only to the extent that private property rights are maintained. Benefit payments rest upon social decisions to tax and redistribute the output that comes from the use of wealth to the benefit of certain people. Both the institution of private property and the system of benefit payments exist in our society because the democratic political process gives them legitimacy. But there are important differences.

It is commonly believed, and I believe accurately, that the system of property rights tends to encourage saving and wise investment, and thus enhances output and general well-being. As presently arranged, the welfare system provides useful services, but probably impairs the longer term performance of the economy as a whole. This is unintended and unnecessary, and later chapters are intended to show how the situation can be remedied. But whether helpful or not, benefit payments are a commitment of part of the national income to giving nonwork income to those who qualify. They *do* get their nonwork income from a claim on the national wealth which is established through the political process, and which bears considerably less relationship to their efforts to add to national wealth than is the case of most recipients of nonwork income. It seems quite appropriate to refer to the effect on the position of the income opportunity line from the receipt of such income as a *wealth effect*.

When nonwork income is raised (or lowered) the income opportunity lines shift upward (or downward) *but retain the same slope*. A wealth effect is shown by the vertical distance between lines like $OW_{1.65}$ to $AW'_{1.65}$. It is most conveniently measured on the vertical axis.

The actual change in the number of hours worked as a result of a wealth effect is referred to as the *income effect*. It involves the juxtaposition between the relevant income opportunity lines and the system of indifference curves. The wealth effect refers only to the change of income opportunity due to a change in nonwork income. The income effect includes the response to the changed opportunity.

Substitution and Tax Effects

Government also affects the income opportunity lines of individuals by taxes and reductions of welfare benefits that are geared to the amount of nonbenefit income received. We will call these alterations in the income opportunity lines *tax effects*. They affect the slope of the actual income opportunity lines that individuals face. The slope typically is flattened making it less attractive to work as much as before. As a result we expect that individuals will substitute more leisure and leisure time activities for former work time. The actual change in the number of hours worked due to the changed slope of the income opportunity lines is called the *substitution effect*.

Most taxes, however, have a double effect. They reduce the total after-tax income as well as changing the slope of the income opportunity line. If individuals have Cobb-Douglas type preference functions, these two effects offset each other only if the tax is a fixed percentage of the individual's income from work and even then only if the individual has no nonwork income. In that case the tax effect is like a reduction of the wage rate. The United States income tax has deductions and progressive rates and so has a complicated effect on income opportunity lines in a given year, and additional effects over time. We do not attempt to analyze the tax effects of such an income tax. Rather, we will focus attention on the tax effects of welfare programs that reduce benefits as more is earned so as to build a tax effect into the welfare programs. For example, the state of Washington provisions, described above, produce an income line shown as a dashed line for a person who earns $1.65 an hour and qualifies for a benefit of $2800.[a] The benefit has a wealth effect of $2800, the rules affecting income from work have a tax effect of 100 percent on the first 1696 hours of work per year and zero thereafter.

For convenience of expression we refer to all aspects in government programs that result in a parallel shift of the income opportunity lines as wealth effects, and all aspects of government programs that affect the slope of the income opportunity lines as tax effects. We will not attempt to divide actual changes in hours worked into those due to income and to substitution effects.

Part-Time Workers

It has been pointed out that less than 10 percent of total output comes from part-time workers. Still, 10 percent is a significant amount, equal to more than two years growth, and programs which would unnecessarily reduce the desire of present part-time workers to continue work should be avoided. Only very limited data exist from which one might infer the shapes of the indifference curves relevant to part-time workers, but there is no reason to suppose that it differs much from the Cobb-Douglas form. The points of tangency between the income opportunity lines and the indifference curves will, however, come at less than 35 hours of work a week, less than 50 weeks of work a year, i.e., at less than 1,750 hours of work a year. It may still be true that well-paid, part-time workers will wish to work the same number of hours per year as more poorly paid part-time workers when neither enjoy nonwork income. If so, and we will assume it to be so, a preference function of the Cobb-Douglas type is appropriate.

The preference maps for part-time workers will be like those for full-time workers, except that the horizontal scale will be changed so the tangencies between the income opportunity lines and the indifference curves where all income is from work comes at 1,000 hours rather than 2,250 hours.

There are, of course, many degrees of part-time work, just as there are many levels of full-time work. Table 2–2 gives some idea of the range. The preponderance of the workers worked 35–40 hours with more than 21 million working longer and nearly 17 million working shorter hours. It is expedient to consider only two groups, one centered on 2,250 hours a year, the number found for the lower income workers where the supply curve goes vertical, and another centered on 1,000.

Several actual and proposed welfare programs are analyzed in the next

---

[a] This case is analyzed more fully in chapter 3.

Table 2-2
Weekly Hours Worked in May 1970

Hours	1–4	5–14	15–29	30–34	35–40	41–48	49+
Number of workers (millions)	0.8	3.9	7.8	4.3	36.5	8.8	13.0

Source: Calculated from data presented in G. M. Moore, J. N. Hedges, "Trends in Labor and Leisure," *Monthly Labor Review*, February, 1971, *94*, Table 7, p. 8.

chapter. The object is not so much to understand the programs themselves as it is to discover why a seemingly insatiable demand for such programs should arise in a period of prosperity when, in the light of changes since 1920, there would appear to be little and diminishing need for them.

3

United States Welfare Programs and Work Incentives

This chapter has two objectives. Its prime purpose is to show that decisions about work are influenced by the opportunities for nonwork income, such as those offered by various social insurance and welfare programs. The analysis presented here is not intended to evaluate them as a whole, but only to show how certain of their characteristics contribute to rising welfare expenditures in prosperous times and frustrate the full employment goal.

The second objective is to show that the characteristics that result in rising welfare costs can be explained without assuming that a growing segment of the population has different moral standards, that is, suffers from a lack of the "work ethic." The unemployment problem is not, as I see it, a moral problem.

One does not easily discover how and where one can make a contribution to output in complex modern free society. There is no political authority to direct idle individuals to build pyramids, water conservancy works, or temples. We rely upon individual people seeking opportunity.

This has not always been true. During most of history individuals had a "duty" to "serve" some individual or group who had authority. Work was a duty. The fact that it was a duty implies that the individual did not wish voluntarily to do as much as he often was obliged to do. The authorities made working an ethical matter, expressing pleasure in good works and imposing sanctions against idleness.

Today, when one feels an obligation to work, there is no one to tell him what to do. We say that he is "unemployed through no fault of his own," and wish to provide him with some minimum level of income. This is done for those who are "deserving," but since there is no one who can direct the person to a specific job, since to do so would violate his freedom and dignity, very serious consequences result from any failure of the system of markets that makes labor costs too high for potential employers, or returns to potential workers too low. Such failure creates unemployment, expands welfare costs, and the expanded welfare costs exacerbate the unemployment problem.

To repeat, what we have is an economic problem, not a moral one. The primary purpose of this chapter is to show that statistical evidence supports the thesis that people respond to wealth and tax effects in ways that produce the problems just outlined.

The Situation

"Welfare"—i.e., social insurance, public expenditures for health and public assistance programs—has grown enormously in the last decade although it has also been the period of highest prosperity and most equitably distributed income in the nation's history. Nevertheless, present programs are considered inadequate and a politically minded president and Congress are preparing substantial expansions. Why? This chapter shows that present programs are double-edged. They improve the income of beneficiaries in ways that magnify real costs and impede extension of aid to those who still are poor. The rhetoric in the press suggests that poverty is something new. It implies a worsening situation for the lower income groups. Objectively measurable evidence of increasing absolute need is not to be found. Instead, the percentage of families receiving less than $3,000 of 1969 purchasing power declined quite steadily from 26.1 to 9.3 percent between 1949 and 1969.[1]

This remarkable success is treated as if it were a failure. Perhaps this feeling of failure exists because a political majority came to the conclusion that the poverty problem was small enough to permit its complete and prompt elimination by extending welfare programs of the type developed in the Great Depression of the 1930s, plus additional public school-type approaches into special education for disadvantaged children, youth, and some adults. The mood of crisis appeared when the problem turned out to be larger than many expected, and apparently increasingly resistant to the chosen means.

The original vision is correct. What was called poverty in the 1960s can be eliminated (but perhaps not what will be called poverty in 1980). But it cannot be done effectively by extending old programs, because the frustrations that are called welfare crisis by some is a product of the wealth and tax effects built into them.

The old welfare programs induce people to act in ways that undermine the effective productivity of an increasing proportion of the labor force unless countered by costly and humiliating administrative controls. This creates tensions between the built-in incentives and the administrative controls, invites behavior that frustrates the controls, and tends to induce an alien class structure that would not exist in the absence of the programs. These developments impair the growth of the nation's productive base, the taxation of which pays for the welfare programs. Let us see why this is so.

A Generalized Analysis of Welfare Programs

The total welfare program is intended to provide every "deserving" person with a secure minimum income. It amounts to a commitment of the earnings from a portion of the national wealth to this purpose and, in effect, is a conditional redistribution of wealth to those without personal wealth. An income guarantee of $2,000 a year gives the recipient the income of $33,333.33 invested securely at 6 percent.

What about the differences in people's ethic? Little is heard about the work-disincentive of the wealth effect as it relates to middle and upper income individuals who enjoy income from their personal wealth holdings. But much is heard about work disincentives associated with welfare programs. There is a good reason for this. Those with personal income from wealth holdings will wish to work more than those receiving equivalent welfare benefits *if their preferences are identical.* This is true because those receiving income from their own wealth do not sacrifice the income from their wealth (except to regular income taxation) if they earn additional income from work. But those on welfare are subject to a tax effect, and lose a very large part, sometimes all of their benefits when they receive additional income from work. Under the present system, an important function of a welfare administrator is to make sure that those who obtain other income lose part or all of their welfare benefits. This tax effect would make it look as if many on welfare have a different work ethic when, in fact, it was the same. This is illustrated in figure 3-1.[2]

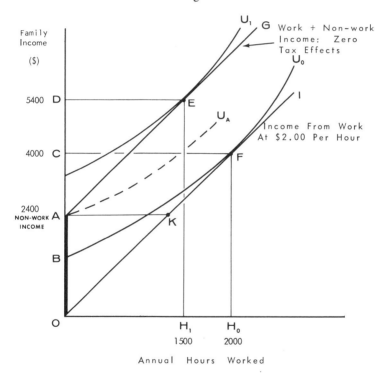

Figure 3-1. Nonwork Income: Tax Effects versus Absence of Work Ethic.

Suppose that three individuals have exactly the same preferences between work and leisure (the same work ethic), and the same ability to earn money. One person is without income from either wealth or welfare. He can earn income from alternative numbers of hours of work as shown by points along his income opportunity line OKFI. Indifference curve BU_0

tells us that he will wish to work H_o hours to earn the income shown by point C (2,000 hours at $2 an hour for an annual income of $4,000) because the best he can do is to attain point F. The second person with the same preferences and the same ability to earn income can, perhaps, qualify for welfare benefits in the amount of $2,400, shown by point A. If income from work disqualifies the person from welfare, his income alternative line becomes AOKFI, but if $1 is subtracted from benefits for every dollar earned, as is the case for some aid programs, his income alternative line is AKFI. If the individual's indifference curves between work and the things that money can buy has the normal shape shown by AU_A, he will prefer welfare and no work, shown by point A, because the indifference curve AU_A, shown as a dashed line, is the highest one he can reach. It passes through point A but otherwise lies above AKFI at all points.[a] The administrator will feel that he has to contend with a "chiseler" who could work but won't, and may disqualify him from benefits, in which case he would work H_o hours.

A third person with exactly the same preferences and the same access to income from work, but who possesses personal wealth that yields $2,400 nonwork income, equal to the welfare benefit, will add to his net income along line AEG. He will have a positive desire to work 1500 hours to earn $3,000 wage income for a total income of $5,400, as designated by point D. He will have no desire to avoid work and live solely on the income from his wealth, as he would if he were in the position of the welfare recipient, facing income opportunity line AKFI, rather than AEG.

The differences in the amount of work performed has nothing to do with differences in the character (work ethic) of the three people but only with the economic choices open to them. The first person, the one with neither income from wealth nor from welfare benefits may be "overworked" for lack of security. The individual with income from wealth enjoys greater security and works a good deal, but less than the man with less security, i.e., less income from wealth. The individual without wealth but with access to welfare benefits will appear to be indolent, dependent, and a burden to others. An administrative effort to discover that he is able to work and to force him to work by denying him benefit payments is simply an exercise of police power to overcome the equivalent of a 100 percent tax on earnings from work. For he would have gladly worked H_1 hours in the absence of reduction of benefits that make his income opportunity line AKFI rather than AEG. This reduction of benefits, this "tax," denies him the security of the wealth effect of the welfare benefit if he chooses to work. So he works less (not at all in the case illustrated in figure 3–1) as would the others if they were in his situation. It is not a matter of the presence or absence of a work ethic.

---

[a] I am informed by social workers that one or two percent of those who lose a dollar of benefits for every dollar earned do in fact work part time. This is explained in most cases by efforts to secure full-time work at substantially better income. But some people probably like to do a certain amount of work. Thus their preference functions have an initial declining sector which may become tangent to such a line as AK in figure 3–2.

The difference in the choices is an artifact of the welfare system itself. It will persist as long as earnings from work disqualifies the person from a substantial portion of the income available to him if he does not work. It generates conflict between conscientious welfare administrators and their clients and promotes a hostile attitude toward government officials. In so doing it tends to divide society into two classes. We do not attempt to assess the degree of crisis that this modern division of society into classes seems to have produced.[3]

Responsiveness of Welfare Recipients to Economic Incentives

Old Age and Survivors Insurance

Some may think that people in general and the poor in particular are not very sensitive to economic incentives such as those just discussed. Available evidence, however, suggests a highly sensitive response to tax effects.

Benefits paid under Old Age and Survivors Insurance (OASI), or "Social Security," as it is commonly called, are of special interest because they provide a crude test of several of the aspects of President Nixon's Family Assistance Plan (FAP), and of the new rules presently applied to public assistance, which are analyzed in a later section of this chapter. The test is crude, however, because older people have widely different amounts of non-work income available from sources other than OASI, and because they have every level of income earning ability. Thus it is not possible to determine just what their income opportunity lines are like. This is an important complication because those with high income-earning ability will not be affected by the difference that is examined here. It is also true that many of those who wish to work have poor health, and for other reasons prefer part-time work, while others prefer to, and do, work full time. Finally, the most interesting difference in income opportunities, the one which makes it possible to observe the wealth and tax effects on hours worked, is defined by age. The break comes at age 72. This is late enough to have an important effect, increasing, one would think, the percentage of the older group who will prefer part-time work. Despite all this, the comparison is instructive.

Kenneth G. Sander evaluated random samples of data for 99,706 people over 63 years of age covered by OASI in 1963.[4] Approximately half were 63 to 72, and the remainder over 72. Those over 72 could earn as much as they wished without suffering any deduction from their OASI benefits. The younger group suffered no deduction if their earnings were less than $1,200 a year, but had one dollar deducted for every two dollars earned between $1,200 and $1,700, and lost one dollar for every dollar earned thereafter until the total deductions equalled the benefit received. Above that point, of course, they kept what they earned, except that earnings were subject to regular income taxes. These provisions produce income possibility lines such as those shown in figure 3–2. The kinked solid line passing through points C, A, E and B′ shows the income opportunities for annual benefits of $1,000 when the wage rate is $1.50.

In the absence of OASI benefits, the individual's earnings would be found somewhere along line OD′EI, the exact spot being determined by

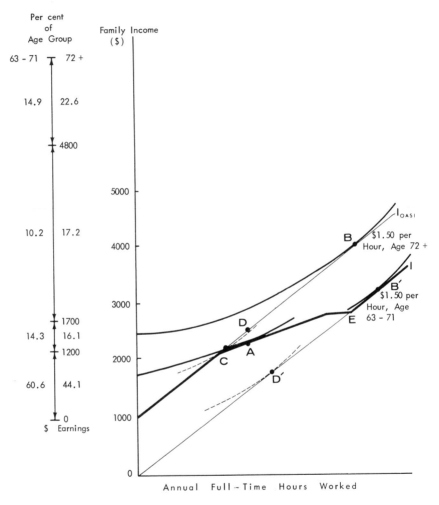

Figure 3-2. Analysis of OASI.

the number of hours worked. The OASI payment has a wealth effect on the income opportunity line, shifting it upward by $1,000 for zero hours of work. There is no tax effect on the hours of work required to earn $1,200 additional (point C on the income possibility curve). Beyond that point, those 72 years of age and older continue to keep all of their benefits and earnings, so that their income opportunity line continues through points D, B and beyond.

A tax effect depressed the income opportunity line of those between the ages of 63 and 72. One dollar is subtracted from benefits for each two dollars earned between $1,200 and $1,700, and one dollar for each dollar earned beyond $1,700 until the full benefit has been recovered. This produces the solid income opportunity line that starts at $1,000 on the axis and proceeds through points C, A, E, towards I.

What behavior is to be expected from this combination of wealth and tax effects? How is the behavior of the two groups, the 63–72 year olds, and the 72+ year olds, expected to differ?

These questions cannot be answered without some reference to the preference functions of those responding to the two income opportunity lines. It is better to be explicit about this. Only those earning relatively low wages are likely to be affected, and a wide variety of preferences is expected. Actual behavior ranges from a large majority which does not work at all, through earnings that range from $200 and less through $4,800 and more. We chose two categories for discussion, full-time workers and half-time workers. The indifference curves drawn to illustrate their preferences are those derived from the Green and Tella data adjusted, as described in chapter 2, to make them conform more closely to the Cobb-Douglas form. The two smooth sweeping solid curves are those consonant with the Green-Tella findings. The more sharply rising dashed lines are similar, but relevant to part-time work. Consider full-time workers first.

In the absence of any program we would expect those who wish to work full time to cluster about point B′, earning about $3,000 for about 2,000 hours of work. Part-time workers would work about half as much and earn about half as much, as illustrated by point D′. In both cases they attain their highest indifference possible under the circumstances.

When a person receives OASI benefits, and there is no tax effect, which is true for the 72+ group, we would expect that those wishing to work full time would work a little less, because of the income effect, as shown by the position of point B slightly to the left of B′. Those who prefer to work part time would also work a little less, as shown by the position of point D somewhat to the left of point D′. In both cases the workers with benefits attain substantially higher indifference curves.

In fact, of course, there is a wide range of preferences ranging from a desire for just a little work to a desire for full-time or even overtime work. As noted above, this reflects differences in health, nonwork income from other sources, and the available wage rate. All tend to produce a wide continuum of desired work experience, but no basis for any sharp break in the number of hours worked, or any bunching at particular numbers of hours.

The column in figure 3–2 shows the actual distribution for 72+ year olds. It provides a basis for comparison with the distribution of earnings of those somewhat younger people whose incomes are subject to the tax effects of the OASI program. Note that a large number, 44.1 per cent of the total preferred to work less than enough to earn $1,200 even in the absence of tax effects. There was no bunching up near the $1,200 level. Note also that almost 40 percent of the total who did work earned more than $1,700.

What is to be expected of those whose earnings are subject to tax effects? Those who wish to work full time will attain a higher indifference curve if they work about half time as shown by the tangency between the income opportunity line and the full timer's indifference curve at point A. This is on a higher indifference curve, and so is better than his situation at B′. The part-time worker is likely to move to the kink at point C since point D is denied him by the tax effect, and he is much better off at C than at D′. It follows that we should expect a larger proportion of workers to want to limit their earnings to $1,700 and less, and to $1,200 and less for the relatively large numbers of normal part-time workers. We should also expect some bunching of earnings in the $1,000–$1,200 bracket (not shown in figure 3–2).

Our expectations are fulfilled. 14.2 percent are found in the narrow $1,000–1,200 bracket as opposed to 6.7 percent of the older group. 60.6 per cent of the younger group earned less than $1,200 as compared to 44.1 per cent of the older group. Only 25.1 per cent of the younger group worked more than enough to earn $1,700, compared to 39.8 per cent of those over 72.

These findings are striking when one remembers that only those earning low wages are likely to be affected in this manner. Tax effects are not likely to affect earnings if wages are as high as $3 when benefits are $1,000. This is shown in figure 3–3. The income opportunity line originating at $1,000 and passing through points E, F, and G is relevant for the 72+ group. Part-time workers will tend to work the hours designated by point F, thereby adding about $3,500 to their OASI benefit, while full-time workers will work as designated by point G, adding about $6,000 to their benefit incomes. The percentage distribution of earnings of people earning that wage probably extends along a broad scale depending upon how much work they prefer or can get.

The younger workers, aged 63–72, face the income opportunity line that also starts at $1,000, but which suffers tax effects that make it pass through points E, H, I, J, and K. They start with $1,000 of benefits, but beyond point I they have all been "taxed" away. Note that the highest attainable indifference curves touch the IJK segment of the income opportunity curve. Even those wishing to work as little as half time are better off although they must return the whole benefit. Some bunching near the corners E and H is to be expected by those who would wish to work less than half time in the absence of tax effects. But the overall tendency toward bunching is less.

In general, the higher the wage rate *relative to the benefit received,* the less will the tax effects affect the earnings from work.

To conclude: the recipients of OASI benefits do seem to respond to the economic incentives built into the program. This is supported by a com-

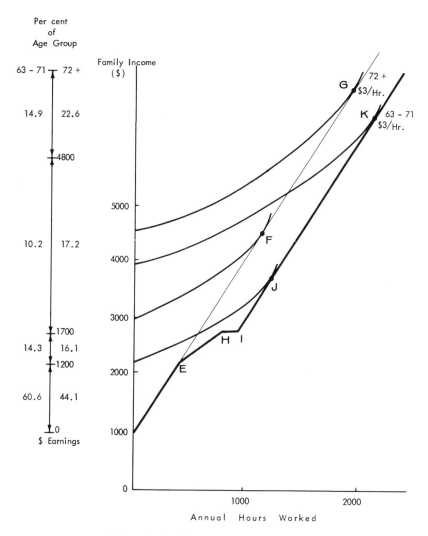

Figure 3-3. Further Analysis of OASI.

parison of the distribution of the amounts of earnings of those subject and those not subject to the built-in tax effects. It is also supported by the halving of the numbers of people of retirement age in the labor force since OASI came into effective operation since World War II.

It would seem foolish to construct expensive welfare programs on the assumption that such responses do not exist. The social cost of this program includes the loss of output that these people would have liked to have made were it not for tax effect built into the program. This cost is left out of account.

Unemployment Compensation

Two studies of unemployment compensation strongly support the thesis that recipients of social security benefits respond to wealth and tax effects built into specific programs. Different states have quite different programs. Raymond Munts' study of the effects of the Wisconsin program is of special interest.[5]

Professor Munts examined the claims of those receiving partial unemployment benefits in the state where a remarkable system introduces two discontinuities into the benefit schedule. The worker can keep 100 per cent of earnings in addition to his entire unemployment benefit up to the point where earnings equal half the benefit, but thereafter only 50 per cent of his unemployment benefit up to another point where earnings equal the full benefit, at which income he is disqualified from all benefits. This produces the segmented income opportunity line, with sharp breaks at points B and C, shown in the top panel of figure 3–4. The indifference curves are those consistent with the Green-Tella data modified to a weekly (rather than an annual) basis.

The income opportunity line was drawn on the assumption that unemployment compensation is one-half the worker's normal full-time weekly earning. The specific values given relate to a regular wage of $2 an hour, $80 a week or about $4,000 a year. Use of the Green-Tella relationships suggest slightly longer hours and greater income at $2 an hour. The indifference curve which passes through the optimum number of hours of work, point A, tells us that the person would be just as happy to receive a little more than $40 a week and not work, as he would be to work full time to earn a little more than $80 a week. It is obvious from figure 3–4 that a worker who can arrange to work just 10 hours a week will reach a higher level of satisfaction (at point B) than he can reach by full-time employment. His choice is between working 10 hours to get $60 and working approximately 40 hours to get $80. His average rate of pay for the 30 additional hours of work during the week is 33.3 cents.

These indifference curves are only approximations of the true curves. But the true indifference curves would have to be very much flatter than these before the individual would find it desirable to choose point A rather than point B.

Note that point C is also preferred to A. A person who analyzes the complexities of the law too late to stop at 10 hours will be well advised to go on to 20 hours. He attains point C at 20 hours, which is on the highest indifference attainable if he has missed his chance to reach point B.

One might suppose that temporarily unemployed people would not or could not respond to such an incentive system. Will they know what their income opportunity lines are? Will they figure out just what they imply? Even if they do, will they be motivated to take advantage of them? And finally, can they control the amount they work so as to take advantage of the situation?

It should also be remembered that there is a maximum limit on the size

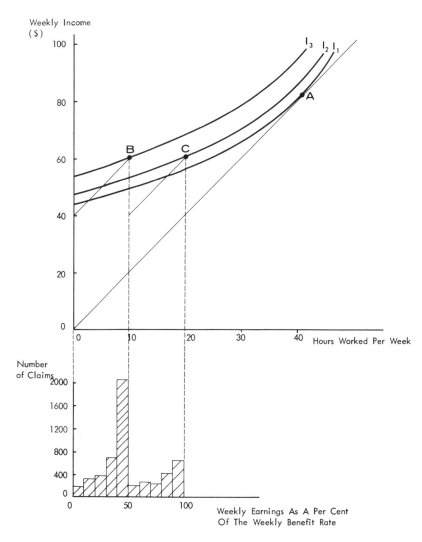

Figure 3–4. Unemployment Insurance Benefits in Wisconsin, 1967.

of the unemployment compensation benefit. People who can earn a higher hourly rate will have earnings that are several times their unemployment benefit, and will prefer full-time work to receipt of partial benefits.

Approximately 108,000 of the 937,000 total weeks of unemployment compensation paid were to individuals who did some work. Munts took a 5 per cent sample of these to see how workers responded. The results are summarized in the lower panel of figure 3–4. Nearly one-third of all instances (2,058 of 6,205) were at point B. More than 36 per·cent (664 of 1,818) of those who worked too much to attain point B in a given week worked enough to reach the next best level, point C. The results appear to be a striking testimony to the predictive power of the responsiveness of workers to the wealth and tax effects built, very likely inadvertently, into this welfare program.

Another test has been made of responsiveness to wealth and tax effects which uses unemployment compensation data. An unemployed person can be expected to spend more time looking for the best job available if his costs of remaining unemployed are reduced by an unemployment benefit. Both the size and the duration of the benefits are important. In general, the size and the duration of the benefits are substitutes, so that it would be reasonable to expect longer job search the higher the average level of benefits for a given duration, and also the longer monthly benefits of a given size may be received.

Gene Chapin tested this expectation using cross sectional multiple regressions which compare the experience in different states over the years 1962 to 1967.[6] He finds that job search is indeed prolonged by higher and/or longer-termed benefits.

Other interpretations of Chapin's results are possible. The size, and especially the duration of benefits is likely to be prolonged in states suffering an unusually difficult employment problem. The cause of the extended benefits could be the long search rather than the liberal benefits. Chapin tested for this and found most of the explanation of extended job search. The strongest influence on the average duration of unemployment is the rate of insured unemployment, followed by the duration of benefits and then the size of benefits as a proportion of the most recently earned wage. We count Chapin's findings as consistent with the theoretical expectation that people change their behavior to take advantage of their economic opportunities. This hypothesis should be placed at the center of welfare reform to avoid undesirable and unexpected consequences.

Public Assistance

The retired and the unemployed may be more responsive to economic opportunities than other welfare beneficiaries, because they are closer to the work ethic. There is some evidence indicating responsiveness of those further removed from the work ethic, specifically recipients of public assistance.

The incentives not to work involved in public assistance should, logically, be a more serious problem than in any of the other programs. This is true because it has very broad potential coverage including young people, and is without any time limit to benefits. Public assistance could fund a permanent nonproductive class.

Figure 3–5 illustrates the position of individuals who have the opportunity to receive public assistance benefits. Consider, for now, only the lower lines in figure 3–5. Line $ODBI_{1.6}$ is the income opportunity line for a person whose income comes entirely from the minimum wage. The highest

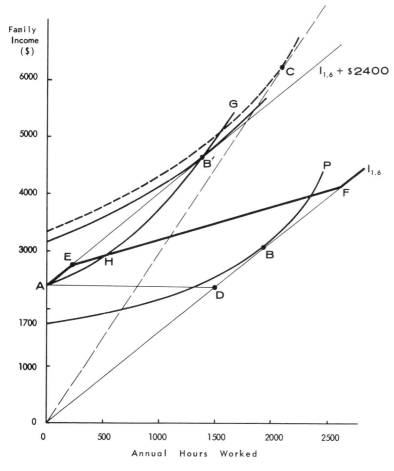

Figure 3-5. Analysis of Public Assistance.

indifference curve which he can attain is P, and B is the most preferred combination between income (about $3,000) and hours worked (slightly less than 2,000). If this indifference curve is correct, he would be equally happy (or unhappy) with $1,700 and no work.

Now if he can receive public assistance of $2,500 a year (point A), he will be better off not to work than he would be working at $1.60, the minimum wage. If receipt of assistance is made a matter of right, or a matter of simply going through the motions of looking for suitable work, he will not work under the terms which are characteristic of public assistance programs. He is more likely to spend his time lobbying to raise the public assistance benefit to something higher than $2,500. As a result, a corps of social workers will be necessary to scrutinize his eligibility, motivate him to improve his skills, and nudge or force him to look for and accept work that he is capable of performing.

The nature of the terms of public assistance programs does make a difference, but it is desirable to notice that when the wage rate is higher, the individual will prefer to work rather than accept assistance on any terms. For example, the same preference structure suggests that full-time work is preferred if the person can earn $3 an hour. The income opportunity line is OC, and the indifference curve tangent to it (at point C) touches the vertical axis at $3,400, well above $2,500. A person capable of earning a $3 wage will not be tempted to stop working to get a public assistance income of $2,500. He would be tempted by any opportunity to receive more than $3,400 for no work.

The tax effect built into public assistance payments affects the decision to work. In the state of Washington in March, 1972, one dollar was subtracted from benefits for each dollar earned if the individual was already working when he applied for assistance and it was found that his income fell below the minimum established for a person in his circumstances. Thus his income potential line was like line $ADBI_{1.6}$ in figure 3–5, and one might expect him to work less, or not at all after qualifying for assistance. A person who was not working when placed on the rolls faced a different opportunity that conformed to national guidelines intended to encourage work. The first $30 of monthly income did not reduce benefits, but benefits were reduced by two-thirds of any income earned in excess of $30 a month. This is shown, converted to an annual basis, as line AEF in figure 3–5.

It is evident that the individual will tend to work only enough to earn $30 a month if his wage is as low as $1.60 an hour unless he has indifference curves that are very much flatter than the ones shown here. No doubt some do, and administrative pressures may induce others to work longer hours. The saving grace, however, is that wages do not have to be very high before an individual will not be interested in a nonwork income as low as $2,500.

If the kink at $30 a month ($360 a year maximum) is ignored, it is evident that the less benefits are reduced to "compensate" for wages earned, the more hours the individual will wish to work. Line AHB′G illustrates the relationship. It is the locus of tangencies between ever-higher indifference curves and ever steeper income opportunity lines that originate at point A (where the benefit payment is $2,500). The "tax" rate is zero at B′. Beyond that point a subsidy given for every dollar earned will induce additional work. The subsidy can be thought of as a "negative tax."

Brehm and Saving made a study of general assistance which seems on the surface to test responsiveness of individuals to payments of the type just discussed. General assistance is similar but is not federally funded, and so it differs widely from state to state.[7] Multiple regression analysis can be used to discover whether or not a larger proportion of families or individuals in a state are covered when the assistance payments are large. Brehm and Saving found that the size of payment and the degree of urbanization were significantly related to the proportion receiving general assistance. They also interpreted the degree of urbanization as indicative of the declining "toughness" of administrators when determining whether or not a person qualifies for assistance.

These results were questioned in two papers. Stein and Albin were, in my judgment, successfully refuted by Brehm and Saving, and in any case weakened their argument by arguing that close administration virtually eliminated "chiselers" who might otherwise be on the welfare roles although capable of self-support.[8]

Kasper is also critical.[9] His multiple regression study introduces many more variables, seventeen in all, and he concludes that differences in labor market conditions, especially unemployment, seem to be the major factor determining the proportion of a state's population on general assistance. Interestingly, the relationship which he did find between the proportion on general assistance and the size of payment suggests that the size of payment makes very little difference once a certain level has been reached.

Kasper, like Stein and Albin, lays considerable stress on the administrative discretion of administrators. Unlike them, he does not see administrators as needed to limit the number of successful applicants for assistance, since he concludes that "it seems hard to believe that disincentives should be a major concern of policymaking in the area of welfare. After all, even the estimated parameters from the log model suggest that higher levels of welfare payments may give rise to continuously fewer additional welfare claimants."[10] Note that this statement of his final conclusions is broad and in context refers to the negative income tax proposal.

Kasper may be correct although one may wonder how he would explain the growth in assistance payments since 1950 in light of the unemployment and participation rates that characterize the period. Moreover, administrative rules and discretion have ample room to affect the number receiving assistance regardless of the number who apply. This materially affects the "cost" of getting on the rolls, and thus the value of the benefits.

In a broader sense, the simple amount of work done is beside the point. The "national objective" is not to maximize work, nor is it even self-support. The social difficulty is one of finding ways to make the preferences of individuals mesh with preferences of others so that each earns and contributes in the ways that are, on balance, most satisfactory to him and most useful to others. Nonwork incomes that come as a transfer from others, desirable and necessary as they are, nevertheless seriously complicate this social difficulty.

Minimum Wage Legislation

Minimum wage legislation is sometimes thought to be welfare legislation. Many people seem to believe that firms which are in business to make a profit should pay a "decent" wage. A belief exists that a firm fails to act in the public interest unless it pays wages at least equal to the minimum.

Just what wage is required if it is to be "decent" is virtually a philosophical question, but the minimum wage has been raised to four times the 1949 level over a matter of eighteen years. As this is written, strong pressure is building in Congress for an increase of at least 25 percent to $2 an hour. It is pointed out that a full-time worker will earn only $3,200 at the present minimum of $1.60. This is less than the public assistance benefit to a small family in many major cities and states.

Little attention is paid to the alternatives available to the workers who have agreed to work for less than the new $2 minimum. The proponents of minimum wages, however, tend to believe that the minimum wage is beneficial to the lowest paid workers. Proponents often deny that the poor suffer greater unemployment as a result of minimum wage laws. This enables them to present the matter as a moral issue that will force presumably well-off employers either to pay better wages or to cease operations, thereby releasing resources and manpower to others who are willing to pay more.

If these beliefs are true, they discredit the model used in this chapter. According to that model the workers tend to be employed by the employer offering the worker the terms that are the most satisfactory to the worker. Making illegal the terms offered by the person's current employer, if they are below the new minimum, sets a chain of circumstances in motion which will tend to hurt such workers and benefit other, somewhat higher paid, workers. Generally, low-paid, nonunion workers will be hurt, and somewhat higher-paid, often unionized workers will be benefited. It is such a mixed bag, that statistical testing of the results of minimum wages has often been confounded with conceptual and data problems.

Yale Brozen seems to have broken through the measurement problems and his study is worth reviewing here. The theory can be stated in this way. Suppose that employers are succeeding in maximizing their profits. In that case they will increase the number of their employees of any given level of ability until the last person of that type hired adds as much to costs as he does to revenues. (This is true because up to that point each worker adds something more to revenues than to costs, and thus adds to profits.) Now generally a job can be done with workers of different levels of abilities. Perhaps they have the same ability while on the job, but those from some easily recognized groups are cheaper to recruit, less likely to report in sick, less likely to quit unexpectedly, more likely to learn the job quickly, or less likely to steal. Or they may actually have different work capacities on the job. Suppose the employer presently employs people at some wage which is about to be made illegal by a minimum wage law.

With the higher minimum wage, the employer must make a decision. Is he going to keep his costs down better by hiring (somewhat fewer) of the workers presently employed, paying the new legal minimum, or will he be better off if he replaces his present work force with somewhat more efficient workers who commanded a wage equal to the new minimum before the new minimum wage law was passed? Relatively, the higher-priced workers have certainly become more attractive, and one must expect a stronger demand for their services, and a weaker demand for the services of those who are able and willing to work for less than the new minimum wage. If so, the higher minimum wage benefits the higher-paid workers and worsens the incomes of the lowest paid (former) workers.

The principal problem involved in testing this expectation is a lack of data on employment rates by wage-rate groupings. It is also very easy to think that one is testing the hypothesis when in fact he is testing something else. Brozen's study has the merit of avoiding the data problem and illustrating the pitfalls.[11]

Data are available for unemployment rates of teenagers by race. It is reasonable to believe that, taken as a group, teenagers are less skilled, less reliable, more likely to quit on short notice, and are generally among the least efficient and lower paid workers in the United States. It is also reasonable to suppose that among teenagers, the less desirable characteristics will be found somewhat more frequently in the nonwhite subgroup. The theory tells us that we should expect such groups to suffer greater rates of unemployment relative to those in the next higher efficiency groups when the minimum wage is increased. But such data do not exist, and it is necessary to use the overall unemployment rate as a substitute. This may not dilute the expected relationship very much because it is always possible that the next best technique uses highly skilled people equipped with sophisticated machinery to replace unskilled people using less sophisticated equipment.

Brozen's procedure is to find the average unemployment rate for all groups taken together, for all teenagers, and for nonwhite teenagers during the twelve months prior to and the twelve months following a change in the minimum wage, and then find the ratio of teenage (and of nonwhite teenage) unemployment to overall unemployment. The expectation is that both will be higher multiples of the overall unemployment rate after the minimum wage has been raised. Table 3–1 collects and presents Brozen's findings. The last pair are not in Brozen's study because data were not available to him then. I calculated the last pair from data that are not quite comparable to his.

Notice the last two columns. Teenage unemployment, and nonwhite teenage unemployment worsened relative to the general level of unemployment, as predicted, in eleven out of twelve instances. The twelfth instance records no change. In that instance, overall teenage unemployment worsened relatively, but nonwhite teenage unemployment remained unchanged at its much higher rate. This may reflect the special efforts that were being made by the Office of Economic Opportunity and other agencies that were subsidizing the employment of blacks.

It is evident that the minimum wage rate increases have been much greater than the increase in prices or wages in general since 1949. The four-fold increase of the minimum wage compares to an increase of 2.9 times in compensation per man-hour in manufacturing industry. So it should not be surprising that teenagers have had greater difficulties in finding employment, and that those among them thought to be riskier employees should have suffered relatively more.

Not merely relatively. Over the period as a whole, while the general level of unemployment was falling from 6.2 to 3.6 percent, and all teen

Table 3-1

Effect of Minimum Wages on Teenage Unemployment Rates

Year	Minimum Wage	Unemployment Rates			Ratio: Teen ÷ All	
		All	All Teen	N-wht Teen	All Teen	N-wht Teen
Fb 49–Jan 50	0.40	6.2	13.9	17.4	2.2	2.8
Fb 50–Jan 51	.75	5.0	11.6	14.8	2.3	3.0
Mr 55–Fb 56	.75	4.2	11.0	15.8	2.6	3.8
Mr 56–Fb 57	1.00	4.1	11.0	18.1	2.7	4.5
S 60–A 61	1.00	6.6	16.4	27.4	2.5	4.2
S 61–A 62	1.15	5.8	15.4	25.3	2.7	4.4
S 62–A 63	1.15	5.6	16.4	29.2	2.9	5.2
S 63–A 64	1.25	5.4	16.6	28.4	3.1	5.3
Fb 66–Jan 67	1.25	3.8	12.6	25.1	3.3	6.6
Fb 67–Jan 68	1.40	3.8	12.9	26.1	3.4	6.9
			White		White	
Mr 67–Fb 68	1.40	3.8	11.0	26.5	2.9	7.0
Mr 68–Fb 69	1.60	3.6	11.0	25.0	3.1	7.0

unemployment was holding more or less steady in the 12 to 15 percent range, nonwhite unemployment rose from about 17 percent to 25 percent. The social implications of this are most serious, but I think that it cannot be fairly said that they reflect increasing racism in the nation. The minimum wage increases have been well-intentioned, but tragic.

It is not hard to see why these conclusions were not reached earlier. Look at the actual unemployment rates for teenagers, columns 4 and 5. The unemployment rate for all teenagers got worse only twice out of six opportunities. It stayed the same twice, and actually got better twice. The nonwhite teenage unemployment rate worsened only twice, but improved four times. It is correct but misleading to conclude from this that raising the minimum wage did not worsen the unemployment rates of teenagers. But it is most misleading because the general unemployment picture was improving and teenagers were not sharing in the improvement. Their relative position was very much affected as we have seen.

Nor did longer periods of adjustment improve matters. Despite mild inflationary pressures and rising wages in the economy generally, the position of teenagers worsened six of the ten measurable times over the periods the minimum wage remained constant. This suggests that given more time for adjustment, a further substitution against teenage employment occurred. This longer term adjustment could, however, be attributable to a decline in the average quality of the teenage labor force due to the increasing numbers who continued their educations because of attributes that also made them the most employable of the teenagers.

The failure to see past the ambiguous changes in the absolute unemployment rates of teenagers is probably conditioned by the moralistic attitude of many who favor the imposition and progressively rising levels of minimum wages. This nourished a bias that is involved in all welfare programs—the notion that there is something cold and inhuman involved in rational calculation that ought to be set aside in these matters. Perhaps this can be described as an "anti-economic" bias. With this attitude, it is easy to look for data that confirms the effectiveness of the minimum wage program. The data on teenage unemployment in table 3–1 can be viewed, if one is uncritical, as showing that the minimum wage increases did not hurt the teenage unemployment and raised their wages.

Negative Income Taxes and President Nixon's Family Assistance Plan

Proposed welfare reforms may be harbingers of substantial improvements as compared to present programs in that they seem to be opening the way to the provision of a minimum income to everyone. In general, however, their wealth and tax effects are unfortunate and will be much more troublesome than the programs discussed previously in this chapter if all poor become eligible simply because their incomes fall below a certain level. The numbers receiving assistance would increase sharply because it is estimated that only one-half, perhaps as few as one-third, of those below the projected minimums are presently able to qualify for assistance under existing programs.

Much can be said for aid to all whose income falls below a certain level, regardless of the reason. Much less administrative effort need be spent in policing the system and more time can be spent to improve the capabilities of those who receive aid.

The principal objection to broad programs is enormous cost. The key difficulty is how to limit aid and still provide adequate support for those who need it. Relatively few will refuse a "free" thousand dollars or so when the cost of his own benefit is spread across the taxes paid by the whole population, and many will use their energies to qualify for benefits if the barriers are modest.

There are only two basic ways to limit the distribution of benefits. One utilizes the police power of the state to prevent those who do not qualify for benefits from receiving any, and to prevent beneficiaries from receiving more than the amount to which they are entitled. They are called "categorical" programs, because one must meet the tests defining some category (being over sixty-five, blind, etc.) to secure aid. Such a system establishes rules which define how people ought to behave, and uses force if necessary to attempt to make them behave that way. Virtually all of United States programs are of this type.

The other way to limit the distribution of benefits is to establish a set of wealth and tax effects that will make the benefits attractive only to some people, hopefully only those who need them. The others will not *wish* to receive benefits under the terms imposed by the wealth and tax effects. Lady Rhys-Williams' "demogrant" proposal in England,[12] President Nixon's Family Assistance Plan, and Professor Milton Friedman's "Negative Income Tax Plan"[13] incorporate this idea, although none of these plans eliminate the need for police power, since individuals can gain by cheating. But a measure of self-enforcement is built into these models. We deal primarily with this type of proposal in the remainder of this chapter.

Variations of the negative income tax proposals and of the Family Assistance Plan have proliferated during the last five years. It is not helpful to present any of them in detail, nor to emphasize specific dollars and cents values on the income possibility lines and wage rates, especially because inflation affects such values. Nevertheless, it is helpful to use specific examples for concreteness, if it is understood that the relationships are what matter, and that the specific values may need to be adjusted. The dollar figures used here are those of a modified Nixon proposal. At the time of writing it seems likely that the family with two children may receive a minimum income of $2,400, plus, perhaps, food stamps. The noteworthy aspect of these programs is that they extend aid more broadly. Lady Rhys-Williams' plan, like Professor Friedman's, would give grants to all who ask for them. The plans differ as to means for holding total expenditures in check, but all reduce benefits sharply as income from other sources rises, i.e., all have pronounced tax effects. The Nixon and Rhys-Williams proposals also make payments conditional on being employed or in training. The tax effects effectively exclude most earners from the program. This is illustrated in figure 3–6 for a Nixon-type program. Income opportunity lines are drawn for two wage rate levels, $2, which seems likely to become the new minimum wage shortly, and $4, the latter to show the self-limiting effect of higher wage rates.

The basic situation, which prevails in the absence of any program, is illustrated for a wage of $2 by the income opportunity line OI, which gives every possible income associated with every possible amount of work, and the specific preference level, AP, which shows every combination of work and income that is as satisfactory as point W, the best level attainable by working.

Under the recent House version of the Nixon plan a family of four with an employable father could get $2,400 base for no work income provided that he stays with the family and either works or takes job training. The provisions of this proposed legislation are complex, and need not detain us here. It is enough to point out that to receive benefits a family must qualify in much the same way as for other welfare plans and that work is among the criteria. This means that administrative decisions must be made, which involve costs, opportunities for unequal treatment, and incentives for individuals to divert their energies from socially useful activities to efforts to take advantage of the system.

When a family qualifies, it becomes the beneficiary of a $2,400 wealth effect. If that is all that happened, the family's income opportunity line would be shifted upward by $2,400 at each level of hours worked (neglecting the effects of other taxes). This is shown in figure 3–6 as the vertical

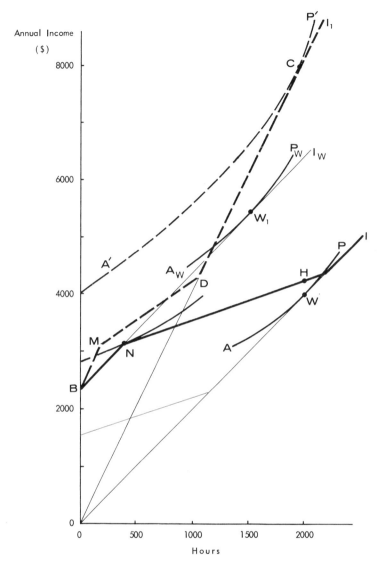

Figure 3-6. A Family Assistance Plan.

distance between the parallel lines OWI and BNW$_1$I$_w$. The income effect of this shift on work performed is indicated by point W$_1$ which is formed by the tangency between the new income opportunity line, BNW$_1$I$_w$, and the highest attainable indifference curve, A$_W$P$_W$. As shown, the family would work only 1500 hours, rather than 2000, and would enjoy an annual income of $5,400 rather than $4,000. The House bill does not permit it to fare so well, however, as they follow President Nixon's proposal and build a tax effect into the plan.

The proposal includes no "tax" (i.e., no reduction of benefits) when earnings are less than $60 a month. After that, however, the House goes the president one better and proposes a tax which takes two-thirds of earnings in excess of $60 a month, rather than one-half as proposed by the president.[b] The tax provisions of the House bill make the family's net income opportunity take the kinked shape illustrated by the heavy line BNHI in figure 3–6.

If the family's indifference curves are reasonably close to the shape which we have found consistent with the Green-Tella data and the studies presented in this chapter, the family will reach the highest attainable indifference curve at point N where only enough work is performed to earn $60 a month. A family head who would have chosen to work 2000 hours to earn $4,000, will be better off although his total income is some $800 less than before. He will work only about 360 hours to earn about $720 to add to the $2,400 available under the plan. Note that the taxpayers provide as much as they would in the absence of any tax effects, when the family would have preferred to work 1500 hours.[c]

The administrator of the program is expected to insist on full-time work as a condition for qualifying for the program. For this reason, the position of full-time work on the kinked income opportunity line is marked with an H. At that point the family receives a net income supplement of only $200. But the indifference curve passing through point H (not drawn) is much lower than the one passing through point N. This tells us that considerable administrative vigilance will be required if that much work is to be performed. Once $60 is earned in a month, every day spent "sick" or "looking for work" is a small victory for the beneficiary over the "establishment" that can be won by using its own rules against it. The administrator's problem is further complicated because other programs exist for families where all of its members are classified as nonemployable.

Tax provisions are important because there are a large number of families who are not now eligible for income supplements and who are presently supporting themselves. It is important that their contribution not be lost by making them eligible for income supplements.

Consider now the second matter illustrated in figure 3–6. It is very important and helps explain why it may be desirable to impose high tax rates in welfare programs despite the unfortunate incentives to low-income earners just discussed.

The high tax rate succeeds in automatically excluding many somewhat more productive workers. This is illustrated by the dashed lines in figure 3–6. They represent the income opportunities for a family whose head

---

[b] Actually the reduction of benefits can amount to a much heavier tax rate than 67 percent, especially when account is taken of supplementary state programs. For example, provisions include withdrawal as income rises of free or subsidized child and medical care, and increased payments for food stamps. These important details are not analyzed here.

[c] Some experimental evidence that suggests a different result is discussed later in this chapter.

can earn $4 an hour. If he works full time he will earn $8,000 annually, as shown by point C, where his highest indifference curve A^1P^1 is tangent to his income opportunity line, OI_1. If this family should qualify under the House plan, its income opportunity lines would become $BMDCI_1$. It is obvious that this kinked dashed line lies below the family's highest attainable indifference curve at every point except point C. This means that the family would not benefit at all from the plan. They would work the same amount and earn the same income with or without the plan. They would not, therefore, wish to take the trouble to qualify for the program.

The indifference curves used here, taken in conjunction with the income opportunity lines strongly suggest that only families with quite low hourly earnings will wish to participate in a program with provisions like these. Those who do wish to participate will prefer to work only a little. The dividing line is in the neighborhood of $3.25 an hour. It should be pointed out that the same general statements can be made for families who can earn up to twice as much per hour if they prefer to work only about half time under normal conditions.

The indifference curves used in these examples may not be correct. If the true slope is flatter, the preferred position will occur on the flatter section of the income opportunity curve, and the reduction of hours worked will be less.

Statistical Studies of the Relationship among Wealth and Tax Effects on Work Performed

There are a number of controlled experiments presently in different stages of completion. There are, in addition, several a priori studies of the probable effects. Only the most nearly complete of the experimental studies is summarized here.

Harold Watts has headed a major experimental study which is attempting to discover the reactions of able-bodied poor to alternative variations of income guarantee plans that include tax effects. His approach is to select people and give some of them (the experimental group) income supplements under such terms as a $1,500 minimum, 50 percent tax scheme, while giving the others nothing (except a payment for submitting to interviews). Both groups are then studied for approximately two years. The third and final year of this study is being completed as this is written, and only preliminary reports have appeared. Those who received the income supplements reduced their hours of work 12 percent, but have increased their wages by 10 percent. This leaves them in the same earned income position as the control group that received no supplements. It suggests that the incentives not to work are small. The summary statement of the preliminary report reads in part, "At this point there have appeared no obvious patterns within the experimental group but that question has not yet been sufficiently explored to warrant rejection of any hypothesis."[14]

The preliminary finding, for which no satisfactory explanation had been found at the time of writing, is higher wage rates earned by the experimental group that offset the loss of income that would otherwise accompany the (expected) reduction of hours worked.

One can hope for much interesting information from the Watts and other studies presently in progress. Many variables are under study such as the number of workers in a family, the stability and ethnic character-istics of the families as well as the effects of the variety of "tax" rates in-cluding rates that vary as earnings rise.

All experimental studies, however, suffer from the fact that the individ-uals know that they are involved in an experiment. Interviews and careful attention have to be paid to what they do. As a result there is serious dan-ger that a "Hawthorne effect" will affect the findings. The Hawthorne effect refers to an early discovery in scientific management that the fact that the workers were getting the interested attention of management turned out to have a much greater output-stimulating effect than the particular process selected for testing.

The surest way to avoid Hawthorne effects is to derive results from past data, such as those utilized by Green and Tella's study. As it happens Green and Tella attempted to estimate the income and substitution effects from a $1,500 minimum income guarantee complemented by a 25 percent and a 50 percent "tax" on earnings which commenced with the first dollar earned. They estimate a 11.5 percent reduction of hours worked, with roughly two-thirds of the reduction the consequence of the tax effect.[15] Their conclusions are similar whether or not the wife works. As expected, the families with higher earning ability reduce their working time less, and part-time workers of a given annual income level reduce their hours by a larger percentage.

Green and Tella estimate the loss to Gross National Product as about $1.2 billion, that is, about one-seventh of one percent of the total GNP for that year. The figures presented earlier in this chapter imply larger losses. This is due in part to the higher income guarantee, and partly to the existence of a kink at the point where the tax rate becomes effective. Indeed, the kink is important largely *because* the minimum is $2,400 rather than $1,500. The light line originating at $1,500 on figure 3–6 shows that the kink lies below the family's highest attainable indifference curve when it can earn $2 an hour and the tax rate is 50 percent or more.

In any case the amount of income lost is small relative to the GNP.

The points to be made here, however, are that substantial incentives to work less are contained in transfer programs that have tax effects: that in general, the tax effects are more potent in reducing the attractiveness of work than are the income supplements, but that the higher the income supplement is, the more potent the tax effect becomes.

Tax provisions tend to raise the cost of the programs because they cut recipients' work efforts by more than the saving to other taxpayers. Tax provisions also reduce the value of the programs to recipients. Attempts to reduce the direct cost of the program to other taxpayers requires administrative effort that tends to divide society into classes, a division that may already be beginning to have serious long-run consequences.

Conclusions

Available empirical studies support the predictions produced by the simple model described in chapter 2. Income opportunities which have been modified by governmentally instituted wealth and tax effects have had the consequences predicted from a system of individual preferences assumed to be substantially the same for all people. Broadened coverage and increased benefits designed to make the programs more adequate also provide stronger incentives to more people *not* to actively seek employment. This increases the burden on administrators. They must be more vigilant and "tough" if those who can are to support themselves. This tends to sharpen the emerging class division in American society.

These conclusions suggest that if we are to get out of the "welfare mess," welfare reform must include changes in procedures that will tend to induce desired behavior rather than undesired behavior that must then be countered administratively.

Part II
Analysis and a Positive Program

4

Individual Decisions and Social Welfare: Toward a Theory of Optimal Employment

We turn now from the matter of individual reactions to opportunities to a much broader and more difficult question. It has several parts. The first is to define optimal responses as viewed by the community, and the second is to ask how optimal responses may be induced when the individuals are left free to make their own decisions in efforts to attain their own objectives.

An Analytical Model

Some notion of an "optimum" is necessary in order to speak of an optimal level of employment. A great deal has been written about the meaning of optimal by highly intelligent and learned men. This literature is a major portion of welfare economics. Most of it requires sophisticated mathematics not appropriate to the level of the discourse used in this book. The analysis presented in this chapter does not go beyond, nor does it contradict, standard welfare analysis. It does, however, apply the analysis somewhat more extensively than usual. We follow sophisticated models by assuming that necessary but here unexamined adjustments do take place, and by limiting analysis to the best understood and simplest "model" of the economy. That model is referred to as the "competitive" model.[a]

Because some readers may feel that these simplifications vitiate the analysis, it is necessary to state why I believe they are mistaken.

The fundamental characteristic of the competitive model is that people do have alternatives. They do tend to choose the occupation, the specific job, the amount of work, and the menu of goods that are most satisfactory to them. If they do, they tend to buy the things that they prefer, increasing the demand for them. Producers of those products are made more financially able to buy additional resources and to hire more manpower. They can offer better deals to working people and suppliers. This affects the decisions of workers and suppliers so that more of these things, and less of others, is produced. The next five paragraphs describe what a firm must do if it is to maximize its profits under competitive conditions.

As long as any employer can hire a person for less than what that person

---

[a] It is possible to make a more formal general equilibrium analysis of the effects of nonoptimal (or inefficient) factor pricing. The simplest formal analysis known to me is placed in an appendix to this chapter. I do not think that comprehension of the more formal analysis is essential to understanding the basic arguments and policy suggestions.

will add to the employer's receipts, that employer will add to his profits (or subtract from his losses) by hiring the person. Thus when equilibrium is reached—when he has hired just the number of workers he wants of a given ability class—the wage paid will be exactly equal to what the "last" employee adds to his employer's gross income. That is to say, the worker will get the full amount which he adds to the receipts of the firm for which he works. Under competitive assumptions, this is equal to the amount added to physical production times the price of the product. Note this exactly: the *full* amount that the final consumers pay is what the worker gets. Under these circumstances the wage does measure the addition to consumer's satisfaction at the equilibrium price.

This analysis must be pressed further. In a fundamental sense every worker is "the last worker hired," for if the work force employed by a firm were diminished by any one worker of a particular ability class, no matter which one, the weekly output would fall by the same amount.

The fact that the workers as a group get less than the total receipts does not imply there is anything the matter with the conclusions of the previous two paragraphs. It only means that there are other costs. The firm must also buy raw materials, power, pay taxes, etc. The quantities of each input that can be bought in greater or lesser amounts are also adjusted until the cost of the last addition is exactly equal to the amount that it brings to the firm in additional receipts.

The analysis must be pressed still further. For a broader optimum the firms must compete so that the returns on their investments, adjusted for differences of risk, are the same. In any given year the returns on their investments (their profit rates) will be different because the economy is dynamic and everchanging. But over time the differences will average out if competitive conditions are prevalent.

Competitive conditions are often taken to include complete knowledge of alternatives and quick and cheap transfer from less attractive to more attractive situations. These are analytically convenient assumptions because they simplify theoretical expectations. We cannot, and do not, make them. Information and mobility are costly, and these costs must be included in our analysis. The competitive model is used to analyze these costs.

Men of affairs have never been happy with analyses that rest on competitive assumptions. Such analyses seem unrealistic because they imply that individual people and businesses have no control over the prices they pay or the wages or other income that they receive from an employer. There is little room for management, and men of affairs think that management and bargaining have very important direct influences on wages and prices.

The strongest defense of the use of competitive theory is that it remains the most powerful and reliable of the available types of analysis for examining the workings of the economy in the large. Most useful knowledge about the economy has been mined from a stubborn political economy with the simple but tough and adaptable tools of competitive theory. Competitive theory has been found helpful even in Soviet-style economies where every important firm is presumably controlled by a state monopoly.

Another defense of the use of competitive assumptions is that there is little discrepancy between its predictions and certain empirical estimates, including those of the loss of satisfaction to consumers ascribable to departures from competition in the American economy. The largest estimate places the loss at 6 percent of national income, and analysis of the statistical procedures used shows even this relatively small amount to be a gross exaggeration. One percent is a more accurate estimate. My own studies show that very few firms can hold their prices as much as 5 percent above the competitive rate for as many as six out of ten years. I found only 30 firms out of *Fortune*'s list of the 500 largest industrials which held prices as much as 5 percent above the competitive rate for as many as six years out of ten during the years 1956–69.[1]

So we use the competitive model in this chapter. According to that model the wage rate represents the contribution that a person makes to the satisfaction of others' wants by working another hour. A person's income from work in a year represents the value of his annual contribution via work to the satisfaction of others' wants during that year. Parenthetically, it should be noted that this conception is a basic building block for the Gross National Product and the other national accounts.

An Individual's Life Cycle under
Optimal Conditions

Before analyzing the existing nonoptimal situation it is helpful to briefly analyze the phases through which a normal individual will pass when conditions are optimal. The four phases are (C) child, when it is optimal if he does not work, (Y) young adult, when good health, ambition, and small resources make work relatively pleasant, but wage rates are likely to be modest, (M) prime age, when remuneration is at its peak, some income is received from nonwork sources (at least equities in house, furniture and car), but when some decline in willingness to work long hours per year may have occurred, and (R) retirement, when income from nonwork sources is higher, income opportunity is less, and the enthusiasm for work has abated considerably. All of these are diagrammed in figure 4–1, with the curves appropriate to each of the four phases lettered in accordance with the phases just described. What needs to be emphasized at this point is that the individuals' and social optima coincide at *each* phase.

As a child a person receives maintenance, education and other attentions that, among other things, prepare him to contribute later. Presumably he has no income-earning potential. Therefore, his income potential is shown as a dot on the axis, C, and no preference function between work and income is relevant. This is optimal in an ideal world because the child is wanted, and the parents have enough emotional stability to keep wanting him.

The young worker is shown without nonwork income, i.e., without as-

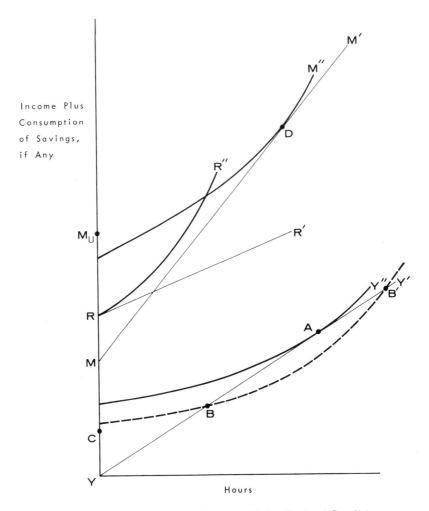

Figure 4–1. Life Cycle Employment Under Optimal Conditions.

sets. This may be an exaggeration of his poverty, but it will do as an extreme case, for he may also have debts, which would start his income opportunity line below zero.

The amount of work done by the young worker is optimal under competitive assumptions. Until he reaches point A he adds both to his own satisfactions and to the satisfactions of others. This is shown in the following way. Consider the situation if he stopped working at point B. At that point he would be on the indifference curve shown by the dashed line which lies below the one passing through point A. Every step up the income opportunity line towards A takes him to a higher indifference curve. Thus the young worker *wishes* to work additional hours at the same wage rate. The amount that he adds to production, multiplied by the price of that output, measures the value of his output. People who buy the output have a free choice of many goods and services and their preferences are such that the quantity of this worker's product put on the market commands that price. There is no better evidence than this that the worker's product has this value to them when compared to all things that they could have obtained with the same funds.

It follows that the worker serves others at a cost to him which is less than the value of his output to others as he works more and more, so as to earn more and more—until he reaches point A.

It is not optimal that he work more hours than that shown by point A. Additional units of output may be as highly valued by consumers as before (as is shown here, since one person's output is too small to affect product prices). But the cost to the worker becomes greater than the value to the consumer as he goes beyond point A. At B', for example, he would be no better off than he was at B when he worked less than half as much, and earned less than half the income.

A social optimum must count the worker's costs as well as the gains in the value of output to consumers. It should be clear that the worker's costs include the subjective costs of fatigue, discomfort, desire for more leisure, as well as the money costs of getting to and from work, special clothes, etc. All of these are taken into account in the indifference curves which show his preferences between additional work and more money income.

When the worker matures and reaches prime working age he will have become more productive. He will have accumulated some assets which yield nonwork income in money or kind, he probably will have insured himself and his assets against some risks of loss. He may feel a stronger desire to work because of obligations, or love of work; or he may feel a lesser desire to work because of reduced vigor, or broader interests. The income opportunity line MM' illustrates the earning possibility of the mature worker. The indifference curve marked M'' is the highest that he can attain. Point D is optimal both for him and for society in a competitive world. The logic is just the same as it is for the young worker as he moves from point B to A, or from B' back to A. The fact that the mature worker has some income from nonwork sources does not change the conclusion. The income from his assets are the result of his saving. They yield a return because they either went to increase the capital stock of the community, and thus enhance the productivity of labor and other factors in the current year, or they were used to finance consumer purchases that could more economically be purchased "early" and bought on time while the item was being used. In either case, the mature worker's savings yield an income because they contribute to current production, so the fact that this wealth effect reduces the amount of work he will wish to perform does not make it nonoptimal. This becomes clearer when the retired worker is considered.

The income line labeled RR' and the indifference curve labeled RR'' represent the optimal position of a retired person. It is also optimal for society. The retired person will have saved enough so that the earnings from his savings, plus, perhaps, the reduction of principal associated with a purchase of an annuity, yields a nonwork income which suffices to make the additional income that he could earn less valuable to him than the time that he can spend in nonwork activities. This result is a compound, in most cases, of reduced ability to earn, and higher personal costs of working even a little. Diagrammatically, this is shown by the fact that the individual's highest attainable indifference curve is either tangent or intersecting his income opportunity line at the vertical axis, that is, at zero hours of work. The result is optimal from a social point of view because the gain to others from his working even one hour is less than the cost to him of working.

Unemployment

A competitive world is not without dynamic change, frictions and lack of information. As a result there are times when an individual will be unemployed. This problem is discussed more fully in the appendix to this chapter and in chapter 5. At this point it should only be pointed out that unemployment can be financed from two private sources in ways that can be considered socially optimal. One source is the employer. The reduction in work force presumably is of some advantage to him, and therefore to the consumers of the products that he produces. It is logical and just that the displaced workers share in these benefits. However, even in the absence of severance pay, or any other direct compensation at the time of job loss, it is reasonable to expect that the history of the various firms and industries will be such as to affect the terms that they must offer to secure the employees that they need. In that case, wage differences will include an allowance that will enable a worker to provide his own reserve against periods of unemployment.

In any case, the worker's own resources provide a second source of income during a period of unemployment. It could be a point like $M\mu$ on figure 4–1 for the mature worker. It is a compound of nonwork income and the using up of assets during a period of job search. This too can be considered optimal although the problem involves uncertainties. He carries on job search until the expected added income to be gained from prolonging the search is of less value to him than the continued cost of searching. This is optimal from a social point of view because the probability that he will find a job which is enough more productive to offset the loss of current output during his period of job search may come at about that point. More attention is given this problem later in this chapter.

"Free" Transfers Cause Nonoptimal
Response and Unemployment

For the moment, assume away those information and mobility problems that result in some "functional" unemployment at all times. Imagine a fully competitive economy in equilibrium in each of its markets and at a full employment position. By full employment we mean that in these circumstances everyone who desires a job at current wages and prices, taking into account existing current welfare rules, has a job; and that every firm has every job filled that it is profitable to fill at current wages and prices.

It is assumed for clarity of analysis that the consensus of preferences of income-earning individuals includes a desire that no adult have an income below the amount shown by point A in figure 4–2. Income earning

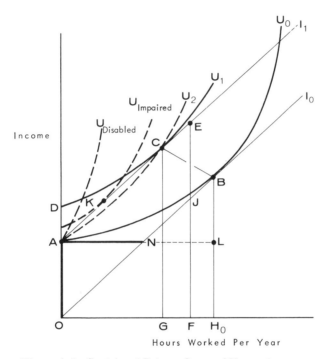

Figure 4–2. Social and Private Costs of Unemployment.

individuals *want* everyone to have at least this much income, and are willing to pay taxes to support them. To simplify matters, it is assumed that no administrative funds are provided to combat chiselers. This might reflect a belief that the administrative costs would be greater than the probable savings from catching chiselers.

Consider now the particular worker two of whose indifference curves are U_0 and U_1 in figure 4–2. He has no wealth of his own. Thus his income potential line is the heavy saw-toothed line $AOBI_0$ (or perhaps, $ANBI_0$ if his welfare payment is reduced by the amount of his earnings until the benefit is repaid). In either case, this man is totally indifferent between welfare payment income A, and working H_0 hours to earn income H_0B.

If he does not work, the taxpayers pay out income A which he receives. If he does work, they pay out nothing, and he is no better off.

Minimum Income or Minimum Satisfaction?

It is now necessary to elaborate the preferences of the income-earners who want to make certain that an income equal to A is received by all people in need.

The income-earners may prefer to give direct charity, but realistically they are more likely to be taxpayers who regard the welfare transfer as a cost that they would like to avoid, and would avoid, if the need were not so great. They do not intend to discourage useful work by the recipient.[2]

These taxpayer preferences appear to be somewhat in conflict. Any effective minimum income guarantee will have some wealth effect that will tend to reduce work effort. But if the taxpayers are sophisticated they will think in terms of preferences rather than absolute amounts of work or income. This means that they do not wish to allow the minimum level of *satisfaction* to fall below that associated with a nowork income of A.

They will recognize that work effort has costs of various kinds, as well as rewards, and would agree that a person working OH hours for H_0B income is no better off than one with the lower income OA, who works not at all.

The sophisticated taxpayer of a liberal disposition might go just a bit further and include among his preferences a disposition to accept, with only a little grumbling, a situation where individuals get to higher preference functions than ABU_0, the minimum preference function upon which points A and B occur, provided that it does not make his taxes any higher than OA.

If the taxpayer takes this last step, it will place the welfare beneficiary in the same position as the recipient of an assured annual income from wealth equal to the annual benefit payment. Willingness to go that far increases the supply of labor from welfare recipients at existing wage rates to an amount that is optimal by the same criteria applied to others. The worker whose preferences are illustrated here will now wish to work G hours for income GC rather than being torn between no work or working H_0 hours. Some may feel that he should work at least H_0 hours but it is not easy to see why the low wage worker without earning assets should be expected to respond less sensibly (differently) to given incentives than do the others in the community.

Welfare Programs Lower the Social Cost of
Labor Below the Cost to an Employer

It is clear from figure 4–2 that under the present system a worker who chooses to work H_0 hours is paid his whole income by his employer. He also adds an amount to gross national product, to others' satisfactions, equal in value to his wages. But he increases his consumption (plus possible saving) above what he would have consumed had he chosen to accept welfare by only BL, that is, by the difference between his earned income H_0B and his transfer income OA. This creates a situation that needs to be looked at very carefully from several points of view.

From the worker's point of view he is no better off in terms of satisfaction. The value of leisure lost, and the other costs associated with working are just barely offset by the added amount of goods and services, BL, received. This additional output, BL, is the *social cost* of employing the worker.

The taxpayer is better off, although his position is rather complex. He wants the beneficiary to have a minimum level of satisfaction no lower than what he could get with an income of OA and no work, and the individual is getting exactly that much. Therefore, the taxpayer is no better off than before so far as his desires for the beneficiary is concerned. But there is the amount OA which he formerly transferred to the beneficiary which is no longer needed to bring him up to that point.

Both the taxpayer and the former beneficiary would be as well off as before, if the amount OA were to disappear forever. The amount OA is, therefore, the *social saving*. It is the amount of net improvement that occurs because the person works rather than being supported by the transfer from the taxpayer. To summarize, the added product of the worker is composed of two parts: the social cost, which is the added output needed to offset the costs of additional work to the individual; and the social saving, which is the net gain that results from his decision to work. It is reasonable to say that unemployment exists in a meaningful theoretical sense as long as it is possible to achieve some social saving by employing an additional person, or by inducing a person to work another hour.

The taxpayer is money ahead to pay an employer any amount less than OA to make sure the man is hired. In this case, the amount can be trivially small because the worker is no worse off when working than on welfare. It is clear that the cost to the employer, the private cost, of getting this person hired is H_0B. This is higher than social cost by the amount H_0B-OA. This is true because at present there is no way for the taxpayer to compensate the employer (or the worker) for coming to an agreement that will save the taxpayer part, or all, of the welfare costs.

This fundamental malocclusion between social and private cost of employment occurs whenever one can elect not to work and accept the support of others. Modern welfare systems have made the costs visible and organized funds in public hands. They did not create the problem. Public and private transfers may be the root cause of what Keynes termed "the trouble" that produces a tendency towards underemployment in market economies. Technically, an "external economy" exists in the labor market.

The "externality" is removed if the conditions are changed so that any point on the contract curve, CB in figure 4–2, is attained. A very small side payment suffices to bring the worker whose preferences are shown in figure 4–2 to an optimum position in the vicinity of point B. But virtually the whole transfer would have been required if his preference pattern had been the one illustrated by the dashed line ACU_2, a curve relevant to an aged person with reduced work capacity.

The externality is *always* removed if the individual is allowed to keep the entire transfer in addition to his income from work. In that case, the retired or disabled person will find equilibrium at point A, the somewhat more vigorous one at point K, and the normal healthy worker at point C. Note that a person who gains less even from the first hour's work than his cost (here termed the "retired or disabled" person) will not work in an optimal system. The dashed curve $U_{disabled}$ shows his preferences. He stays at point A. The taxpayer is no worse off in any case.

It should be noted that the conditions for an optimum are met. The employer pays each worker a wage that is equal both to what he adds to the value of output and to the worker's "disutility" from his final hour of work. The value of the worker's time to himself is reflected in the additional cost of his work to the employer. This, in turn, is equal to the price paid by the worker-consumer for the final product.

But the total wage paid by the employer is less than the total income received by these workers. They receive an additional "rent," equal (at the maximum) to OA, which is sufficient to overcome the externality caused by their opportunity to receive some income without working.

Administrative Problems: The Advantages
of Broad Coverage Linked to
Zero Recovery Rate

The individual whose choices are examined in figure 4–2 has qualified to receive payments equal to OA. Presumably he would not qualify if it were known that he could earn an income of H_0B by working OH hours. So it is not in his interest to let it be known.

There are grave difficulties involved in the idea that citizens must "qualify" for welfare payments. Rules that qualify some and disqualify others must contain a degree of arbitrariness. They promote a division of the population into opposing classes. They also provide incentives not to work when both the potential worker and others in society could be better off if he worked. The modification implied by the foregoing analysis, that the taxpayers compensate either individuals who have qualified for benefits or their potential employers in order to get them employed, has the disadvantage of inviting fraud.

A fraudulent scheme would work this way. The employer and the worker would conspire to lay off the worker, get him qualified for some kind of benefit, and then hire him back, with the employer and the employee splitting the inducement.

These problems can be avoided if the program is made entirely general. Generalized programs are not unknown to the health, education, and welfare field. Education is provided to all without any means test or other system of qualification for benefits.

Unlike the welfare system, the school system has tended to unite the different social groups. Among the school system's most serious problems are those related to the very class divisions and consequent attitudes of children and parents that have been accentuated by the welfare system during the last twenty years of prosperity.

If the main objective of the welfare system is to provide a minimum income, there is little to be said for maintaining a variety of different programs related to diverse causes of low income. It is better to follow the negative income tax philosophy and provide transfers in accordance with income size alone, after adjustment for family size and the other elements that go into the determination of taxable income. The great merits of the negative income tax are its broad coverage and nondiscriminatory rules for qualification.

The greatest demerit of the negative income tax relevant to the present analysis is the pronounced incentive to work less shown in chapter 3. Many full-time workers who are presently excluded from welfare benefits will wish to work many fewer hours when they become eligible to receive negative income tax benefits and must pay high marginal "tax" rates. The Nixon Family Assistance Plan will encourage low income people to earn no more than $60 a month because of the 50 percent recapture (or "tax") rate of income earned in excess of that amount.

As noted above, these difficulties are minimized if the rapid recapture of the nowork basic income is dropped. But if rapid recovery is dropped another equally troubling problem is created. Costs will increase enormously because everyone will find it in his interest to qualify. Either these high costs must be met somehow, or administrators must be relied upon to interpret and enforce laws that limit aid to those in need. We return to this problem, and to the matter of financing the transfers in chapters 5 and 6.

Toward an Optimal Demand for and Supply of Labor

The welfare system is not the only reason why private and social costs of labor differ, i.e., it is not the sole cause of the externality in the labor market. Unemployment problems arose in specialized economies long before welfare programs, or even before personal charity became substantial.

Two other reasons are important and are part of standard economic literature. One is the cost of information as it applies to the labor markets, and the other is that complicated congeries of conditions that determines the cost of capital goods to firms in the Keynesian analysis.

To the extent that these externalities add to the discrepancy between private and social costs of labor, successful policy to eliminate unemployment must take them fully into account. Information costs are considered first.

Information Costs as an Explanation
of Unemployment

Stigler and Alchian have developed and applied a theory of information to labor markets.[3] Characteristically, they use theory positively to explain observed phenomena. Alchian uses his theoretical construction to explain the unemployment levels of the Great Depression. The fact that he does not fail to explain it suggests that private costs of individuals seeking jobs and of employers seeking employees may have been quite at variance with social costs.

According to information theory, individuals seek job opportunities and prospective employers seek employees until the expected gain from further search does not appear to them to be worth the additional effort. Rational outcomes include decisions to accept prolonged unemployment and unfilled vacancies. The level of employment is, nevertheless, privately "optimal" because it does not pay any decision-maker to choose differently. It is not a welfare optimum if the costs of information to the unemployed and to the potential employers are higher than the social costs.

The true optimal rate of employment is not attained until the equilibrium rate occurs *with all feasible devices in operation that can rectify private costs with social costs.* A feasible way more nearly to harmonize private costs with social costs is presented in the next chapter.

Keynesian Analysis and Policy

Keynesian macroeconomic theory has dominated Western economic thought since the mid-1930s, and Keynesian policies have been part of the standard kit of tools for domestic statesmen for twenty years. A wealth of experience reveals the strengths and weaknesses of the Keynesian approach. Fresh thinking, such as that presented in this chapter can benefit by comparison to the great body of thought and practice which is subsumed under the heading "Keynesian Analysis and Policy."

Keynesian Policy. Keynesian policy probably reached its apogee in the middle 1960s when a strategic tax cut, engineered by the Council of Economic Advisors under the chairmanship of Walter Heller and recommended by President Johnson, achieved the predicted result of reducing the unemployment rate to less than 4 percent.

Experience since the mid-1930s, when Keynesian "new economics" began to have influence, strongly suggests that short-run policy always faces what may be called a "trilemma." Attempts to reduce unemployment "too much" by Keynesian means (i.e., expansionist fiscal policy plus a readiness to hold interest rates to low levels by expanding the money supply) always threaten to produce unacceptable increases in prices and wages. Some people believe that the threatened inflation can be contained or prevented by direct wage and price controls. Thus policy faced three unpleasant choices: higher than "necessary" unemployment, more than "necessary" inflation, and/or the imposition of onerous direct controls. Experience based on the Great Depression, two wars that included wage and price controls, and several postwar mini-depressions, some of which produced unemployment rates of 7.5 percent, suggest that policy can avoid any two of the horns of the trilemma (the unpleasant choices), but not all three. One can view the economic history of the period as a succession of choices that usually moved us from one pair of horns to another. We could, and did, spend some time lightly impaled on all three horns. Unfortunate policy involves being really gored by more than one horn at a time. Terrible policy involves getting gored by all at once.

The Heller-Johnson success brought unemployment rates down a full percentage point to 3.8 percent and increased the rate of increase of consumer prices (as measured by the Consumer Price Index) from about 1 percent a year to about 3 percent a year in spite of a "guidepost" policy which may be viewed as the mildest form of wage and price control. This is a good example of finding an "acceptable" rate of inflation, and a "tolerable" amount of interference that permitted, at least for a time, a "full" level of employment.

Not that the 3.8 percent unemployment rate was defended as desirable in a more fundamental sense.

Keynesian Analysis. Keynesian policies should not, however, be confused with Keynesian theory. His theories do provide a basis which, if correct, could be used to construct an optimal theory. In my opinion, the most acute analysis of Keynesian theory is provided by Axel Leijonhufvud. He finds the same kind of discrepancy that we do between the social and private costs of labor and capital goods to employers. But Keynes' explanation of the cause of the discrepancy is very different from ours, and the techniques needed to improve matters are even more different.

Leijonhufvud summarizes Keynes' basic conclusions:

The "trouble" arises from inappropriately low prices of augmentable non-money assets relative both to wages and consumer goods prices. *Relative prices are wrong* [p. 46, Leijonhufvud's italics] and: Asset prices are wrong and it is to asset markets that the cure, if possible, should be applied.[4]

To repeat, according to Leijonhufvud, Keynes believes that an inappropriate ratio of asset prices to wages leads to unemployment because asset prices are too low. The contention of this book is that the ratio is nonoptimal because wage costs to the employers are too high.

According to Keynesian analysis, there is a tendency to overuse capital assets relative to labor which results in an aggregate demand that is insufficient to use the labor force fully. This can be explained in the following way. Individuals have a tendency to save too much because they respond to incentives to save other than the monetary gain from interest receipts. This oversupply of funds, continually augmented by reinvestment of past savings, tends to produce relatively low interest rates. As a result, firms wishing to expand production can borrow at low rates making the net cost of capital goods low relative to the cost of labor.

A firm, especially one subject to competitive pressures, must attempt to keep costs down. When the cost of capital goods is depressed, a rational firm will use relatively more of the cheaper capital goods where possible, and relatively less of the more expensive labor. But this tendency to use relatively more assets will not, Keynes believes, drive asset prices up to the equilibrium ratio with wage rates. This is true because the total demand for goods and for the factors that produce them is too low.

Keynes' remedy for this shortcoming is, basically, to expand the demand for capital goods. This is supposed to have a two-pronged effect. It should increase the prices of capital goods and should also increase total demand for consumer and other goods by some multiple of the increased expenditures for investment goods. Consequently, total employment is increased. If the policies are pursued with sufficient vigor, full employment is attained. Keynes does not tell us, however, how to know when the optimum ratio of labor to capital costs has been attained.

It is not entirely clear that Keynes' emphasis upon increasing the demand for assets rests primarily on an analytical conclusion that factor prices need to be rectified by increasing asset prices rather than lowering the wage rate paid by the employers. His keen sense of what was possible at the time strongly favored action to increase aggregate demand by using monetary and fiscal tools. Even the control of the money supply so as to lower interest rates, plus the use of government spending and taxing authority to increase government purchases and to reduce personal saving—relatively familiar tools of government—stirred controversy enough.

Keynes and others agreed that it was not politically or economically feasible to attempt to lower money wage rates. He argued that lower money wage rates might not work even if ways could be found to push them down. But he believed that a fall in real wages, brought about by price increases in excess of wage increases, could play a helpful role in attaining full employment.

Inflationary Bias Predominates When Factor Price Ratios Are Improved by Expanding the Demand for Assets. One relatively minor Keynesian approach tends to raise capital good pricing by reducing the supply of savings. The provision of social security, unemployment compensation, etc., reduces individuals' need for savings, and tends to reduce the supply of assets. This will raise asset prices if demand is constant or expanding. Aside from this minor weapon in the Keynesian arsenal, Keynesian policies call for the expansion of the demand for assets, and therefore tend to be inflationary. Common examples of such policies are efforts to produce low interest rates, government mortgage guarantees to stimulate investment expenditure and the purchase of housing, high government expenditures for goods and services and tax reductions intended to stimulate consumption expenditure. The increase in the quantity of assets should increase labor productivity, thereby shifting the demand for labor upwards. As a result, employment and aggregate demand should, in the Keynesian analysis, rise to the full employment level.

Keynesians expect asset prices to rise partly because the capital values of their income streams (their market values) rise when interest rates are forced down, and partly because the demand for productive assets rises as total output expands.

Keynesians do not expect wages to rise much until full employment is closely approached. This expectation was perhaps hoped for more than truly expected, since, at least in the United States, wage rates rose rapidly during the mid-1930s, although the unemployment rate exceeded 15 percent.[b]

The absence of criteria defining full employment is an outstanding weakness of attempts to apply Keynesian analysis.[c] As noted earlier, the tendency has been to define full employment as the highest level possible without "too much" inflation or "too much" direct government regulation of prices, wages, and related matters. This makes the best level of employment dependent upon the discovery of criteria that define the optimal rate of inflation and the optimal amount and kind of intervention. Theorists have found criteria for neither.

Full employment vs. inflation. A major part of the uncertainty about the best full employment goal probably rests on ignorance of actual consequences of Keynesian-style policies that seek to reduce, or maintain, low unemployment rates while also causing inflationary price rises. Neither the analytical nor the statistical problem is negligible.

Even the measurement of price level changes is clouded. Improvements in product quality which result in somewhat higher product prices can mean lower "real" prices. This is most obvious where durability is involved. A 10 percent higher price may buy a product with 50 percent longer service life. It is hard to make even this kind of adjustment in a price index. It is much harder to compare the "qualities" of cars, physician services, and the like over time. Still, given our other troubles, this is a relatively minor problem.

The basic difficulty is much more troublesome and disagreement about it is fundamental. Some argue quite persuasively that there simply is no longer term tradeoff between lower unemployment and rising price levels.[5] The argument goes back to considerations that influence the calculations of the millions of workers, consumers, investors, savers, and businessmen. Gordon and Hynes agree that these decisions are influenced in the short run by monetary and fiscal policies that change the money supply and aggregate

---

[b] On the other hand, rising wages may have been attributed to government policies favoring labor union formation and collective bargaining.

[c] Attend to James Tobin as he defends Keynesian theory and policy in his presidential address before the American Economic Association, "In the nature of the case there is no simple formula—conceptual, much less statistical—for full employment", "Inflation and Unemployment," *American Economic Review,* March 1972, 62, p. 18.

expenditures. But the initial responses that result in less unemployment are offset in the longer run so that the average level of unemployment over time is little affected.

The economic history of the United States seemingly supports the Gordon-Hynes conclusions.[6] The data presented in figure 1–1 suggest that the average U.S. unemployment since World War II is no better than that from 1900 to 1929. But holding the line can be considered a substantial achievement for reasons given in chapter 1. But against that position one must recognize that generally stable prices prevailed before World War I, and falling prices during the 1920s. This compares unfavorably to the troublesome price increases experienced since World War II. Nor was there evident widespread feeling before World War II that wage increases as high as 10 percent a year were necessary to avoid declines in income after adjustment for price changes. It is a fair inference that Keynesian policies have not reduced unemployment rates much, but may have contributed significantly to inflationary pressures.

Persistently increasing price levels create expectations of further increases that build in a demand for escalating wages in wage contracts, increases which employers feel that they can agree to pay. There is increasing evidence that behavior will support the theory that full adjustment is made to *expected* increases in prices. If this happens, the effort to raise asset prices relative to wage costs by inflationary techniques will immediately produce large wage increases and so will fail to lower the unemployment rates as much as expected.

If wages rise as fast as asset prices, the trouble, seen by Keynes, is not overcome. The basic disharmony in factor price ratios remains, and with it, a particular level of unemployment. Policies that expand the demand for assets effectively reduce unemployment in the short run when price increases are not expected, so that wages rise not at all or only a little. But in the long run they inflate all costs and prices more or less proportionately and do not reduce unemployment.

The basic difficulty with policies based on the Keynesian analysis is that no mechanism exists which can be relied upon to change the *ratio* of factor prices actually paid by public and private decision-makers who properly believe that their task is to use the command of resources entrusted to them as efficiently as they can.

Wages and price controls not helpful. The standard attempt to save this situation (aside from futile moralistic complaints that people should not act to satisfy their "selfish" wants) has been to advocate wage and price controls. Wage and price controls certainly have a strong surface appeal. Those who believe that government can make people act against their own interests build a modest logical case for such controls. On one hand, it is said, that if firms would not raise their prices, the price level would not rise. Then the increased spending, created by government, would go to employing more people to produce more goods and services rather than being "wasted" in inflation. On the other hand, some say (or rather whisper) that if wages were held down, prices would not rise. The same expansionary effects on employment and on production, rather than upon prices, would then result from government-induced increased spending. Politically it is better to avoid this chicken or egg argument and advocate controlling both wages and prices.

It is hard to find any example at all of successful wage and price controls. Even totalitarian nations (such as the USSR from 1932 to date) with either national ownership or tight controls clamped on every major segment of the economy find their powers unequal to the task.

Summary. Keynes' vision, that the tendency toward unemployment lies in inefficient factor price ratios is, I think, correct. He is also correct in his belief that asset prices are too low relative to wage costs to employers. But his prescription that asset prices be raised is not now correct, if it ever was. The emergence of inflationary trends in Western economies since World War II tells us that the difficulty no longer is one that can be corrected by raising asset prices by expanding aggregate demand.

Instead it is necessary to find ways to make the factor price ratios optimal by reducing the costs of labor to employers. Quite different tools are required for this task. (It bears repetition that this does not mean that the money income of workers should be reduced.) Chapter 5 deals with this central problem.

Appendix

A Factor Mispricing Theory of Unemployment

An awkward logical problem confronts anyone who wishes to define "unemployment" in a way that is consistent with the theories of the firm and of the household. A person is commonly defined as being unemployed if he is willing and able to work, actively seeking work, and not employed. But what is meant by "willing" and "actively seeking"? It is not expected that he look twenty-four hours a day, or that he accept a job at $1 an hour if he has recently earned a $5 wage. When a person is unemployed (in the conventional sense) he may be bending his efforts intelligently to finding the best available job opportunity at the most reasonable cost to himself. Added job search is expected to turn up better offers, but at greater cost. Thus the "unemployed" person might better be said to be "employed in maximizing his net returns from job search."

Is it possible for unemployment to exist if each "unemployed" person is fully occupied in optimal job search? He achieves (subject to appropriate adjustment for risk) equal marginal utilities per dollar expended on each good and service, between goods and services and leisure, between leisure and the search for a better job, and between marginal amounts of time spent in each leisure time activity: sleeping, eating, recreation, and so on. For the individual the last few minutes spent on each activity, nonmarket as well as market, yields the same addition to well-being. How then can he be unemployed? He does not choose to look harder than he does. He does not offer to work for less than he offers. In short, he is doing what he prefers. Why should he be more willing, or more actively seeking, than he is? And if he isn't, is he unemployed in any fundamental economic sense of the term?

I think that he may be unemployed in a fundamental sense, but it is hard to crack through to just what that sense may be.

Suppose that factor prices are somehow "wrong." Why should that cause unemployment? Were wages lower (or higher) each individual would readjust the amount of labor performed in the market, the amount of job search he would undertake, the quantity of goods he would buy, etc., until all of the marginal equalities are obtained. He might work more or less, but, if it is less, there is no obvious reason to say that he is partially unemployed.

Statements essentially like those just made about the households also apply to business and government decision-making units. They too will adjust the size of their operations, the quantities of the various kinds of labor, capital and resources used, and so on, until the marginal equalities are obtained, subject, of course, to information costs and foreseeable risks.

It follows from this that it is not possible to rigorously define unemployment in terms of the theory of the firm or of the household when one takes

85

for granted the adequacy of the existing laws of property and ability to contract. Put another way, it is not possible to define a person as being unemployed without reference to the impact of the level of his productivity upon others. Unemployment (or overemployment) exists when labor contracts fail to give adequate weight to all of the costs and benefits which are in fact associated with them. Specifically, unemployment exists when defects in the basis for contracting cause the wage rates to which employers adjust to be higher than the net wage rates to which the employers adjust. As a result, both the quantity of labor demanded and the quantity of labor supplied are too little. An external *economy* exists in labor markets.

It is not obvious why this discrepancy should be felt as a threatening social problem when each household and each firm is in equilibrium, and none have influence over the general level of wage rates. Other inefficiencies do not evoke intense reactions. We have found that social pressures to reduce work effort are built into the most widely supported social welfare programs such as Old Age and Survivors Insurance, Unemployment Compensation, Public Aid, and Minimum Wage Laws. Nevertheless, there are at least two reasons why the unemployment problem is seen as acute. The dynamic nature of modern economies produces an unwelcome amount of job-shifting and job-search. The society as a whole has come to play a large role in providing minimum incomes for those who are not employed for one reason or another. Consequently, when individuals step outside of their roles as managers of their individual households or their firms to evaluate the performance of society as a whole, they perceive the imbalance between the household and the market sector. Firms do not find it profitable to hire sufficient numbers of people, and individuals do not try hard enough to be self-supporting.

The tension between rational decisions made by individual households about working and by individual firms about hiring are in conflict with the decisions and opinions of individuals and entrepreneurs in their roles as citizens. As citizens people formulate policies and expectations that put pressure on individuals to seek work more intensively than they feel to be worthwhile and upon firms to hire more manpower than they can afford. One result of these social pressures is to make a good job valued in part for noneconomic reasons—as proof of manhood or independence, as a sign of success, or even of divine favor.

As long as the tension persists, jobs will be sought for themselves, and not for what they do by way of producing desirable goods and services. The problem of unemployment policy is to bring private and social costs into line with each other.

Harry G. Johnson developed a technique, which he attributes to K. M. Savosnick,[1] that can be modified in order to analyze the unemployment problem.

His model is a two-factor, two-good model in which the total supply of the two factors, labor and capital, are fixed. One good is labor-intensive, the other is capital-intensive. Both goods are produced under competitive conditions. It follows that the firms in both industries will be led by factor prices to an efficient use of resources. At such points the ratio of the marginal product of labor to the marginal product of capital is the same in both industries. The ratio is also equal to the ratio of the price of labor to the price of capital.

Johnson demonstrates that nonoptimal equilibrium occurs when the factor price ratios differ for the two industries. The firms in both industries are misled by the wrong factor prices to use the factors in inefficient proportions.

The Johnson-Savosnick model is relevant to the unemployment problem if the two output sectors are redefined. Let one sector stand for the whole market sector and the other for the whole household sector. All human time originates in the household sector. Much time is used for sleeping, eating, recreation, and to produce goods and services used by the household that produces them. We follow traditional usage and refer to all hours spent in the household as "leisure." Households also sell a substantial amount of time to government or private enterprises for a money income which is used to purchase goods and services on the market, to pay taxes, and so on. These hours are referred to as "work" or "labor supplied."

Presumably, each member of a household uses his time to get the most out of his life. This is another way of saying that the last few minutes spent in each activity (or inactivity) adds the same amount to his well-being. The division of time between the household sector taken as a whole and the market sector is decided on the same basis. That is, the individual divides his time so that the last few minutes spent in the market adds the same amount to his well-being as the last few minutes spent in the household sector.

The individual is misled, and makes a less than socially efficient division of his time if the return that he receives from the market does not reflect faithfully his opportunity costs to the community. Typically, the wage rates in the market sector are substantially above social opportunity costs for reasons given in chapter 4.

In general, the value of a marginal hour of labor used in the household sector (the implicit wage rate there) is less than the wage rate paid by the firms. This is true for two reasons. First, because the value of goods produced in the household sector, and the pleasures from leisure, largely escape income, sales, and other taxation. Second, the money wage which firms must pay to attract labor is generally higher than the net value received by the families, especially when potential loss of welfare benefits are at stake. As a result it is rational to use labor in the household sector to do things which add only a little to satisfaction, as compared to what is contributed at the margin in the market sector. In this sense, much household labor is inefficient even after taking fully into account the pleasures from "doing it yourself."

This does not imply irrational behavior by either the households or the firms. The discrepancy in rates of return to labor hours in the two sectors is due to faulty government policies that raise the marginal private cost of labor to firms above the marginal private cost of labor to households. This makes the private cost of labor in both sectors different than its social cost.

A Diagrammatic Model

The foregoing provides a foundation for the formal model presented in this section. The analysis utilizes a diagrammatic model (figure 4A–1) which is essentially a copy of Johnson's.[2] It differs in two respects. The first difference is that the two output sectors are (1) production in the household for household consumption, and (2) production in the market sector where inputs are hired, and the output is sold. The second difference is that Johnson's highly compressed diagram is separated into two panels so as to make it possible to put only one item (an input or an output) on each axis.

Begin by studying panel A, which is called an "Edgeworth Box" after its originator. The dimensions of the box denote the quantity of resources available, here indicated as 100 (percent) for both capital and labor. The quantity of capital utilized by the market sector is read from left to right on the lower horizontal scale of panel A. The quantity of capital utilized in the household sector is measured from right to left on the upper horizontal scale of panel A. A vertical line drawn across panel A will show the division of all of the available capital between the two sectors. For example, the vertical line passing through point P shows 70 percent of capital going to the market sector, and 30 percent to the household sector.

The number of labor hours is measured on the two vertical axes. The percentage utilized in the household sector is measured upwards on the left hand axis, and the percentage utilized in the market sector is measured downwards on the right hand axis. Any horizontal line drawn across panel A will show a specific division of labor hours between the two sectors. For example, the horizontal line which passes through point P denotes 60 percent to the household sector and 40 percent to the market sector. Every point inside of the Edgeworth Box indicates some specific division of both labor and capital between the two sectors.

There is a specific amount of output in each sector that is associated with every point inside of the box. Just how much will depend upon available technology. We follow the usual assumption that at the moment the whole range of technical choices are fixed.

The problem of analysis then becomes one of finding the combination of inputs (labor and capital) that will produce the "best" combination of outputs (household goods and market goods). By "best" we mean the combination that satisfies the greatest amount of human wants.

There are very serious definitional and logical problems involved in "the greatest amount of human wants." They cannot be explored in any detail here. The approach used rests on the same competitive basis that was explained in chapter 4. According to that analysis, each individual will work in the market sector until the added value of the things that he can buy from an additional hour's work just suffices to overcome the costs and subjective burdens involved in working that hour. If the market is working perfectly, the value added to others' satisfactions will then be exactly equal to the costs (of all sorts) to the individual. To work more would cost him more than it would benefit others; to work less would cost him less than it

89

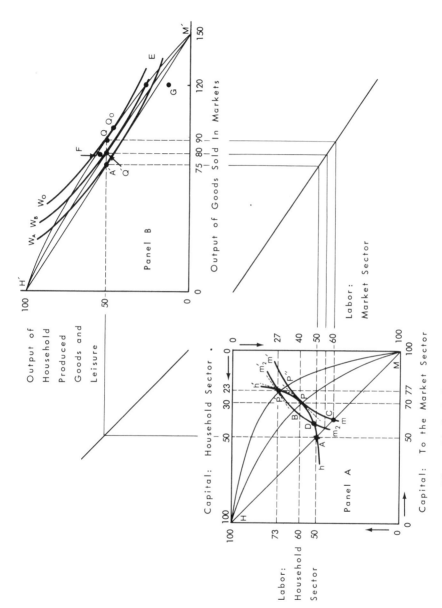

Figure 4A-1. A General Equilibrium Analysis of Unemployment.

would benefit others. He is at an optimum, so far as the market sector is concerned.

It will not be an optimum if the last hour devoted to the market sector carries a higher value to others than the value that he will receive from that same hour devoted to household tasks, or to leisure.

The search for the optimum point inside of the box is made in two steps. The first step is to find a whole series of optimum points, one for each possible combination of outputs. The second step is to find the best point on this "line of optima" (or "efficient locus").

Strictly speaking, the second step is not necessary for the purposes of this book. The first step is sufficient because no matter what combination of outputs is most desired, the input combination will not be on the line of optima when the factor price ratios are not the same in both sectors. The firms and households will not be led to an efficient use of resources unless the prices of labor and capital are the same to the household and the market sectors. We have already given sufficient reasons for believing that this condition is not met.

The efficient locus is illustrated in panel A by the bowed line HPM. Line HPM is composed of all of the points of tangency between isoquants, only three of which are drawn in. They are labeled hh′, mm′, and m_2m_2'. An *isoquant* is a line that shows every possible combination of inputs that will produce a particular amount of some output. Two sets of isoquants are involved in panel A. One set shows increasing levels of output in the household sector. Its zero output level is at point M and it "rises" toward H where all production is in the market sector. Only one isoquant from this set is shown, hh′. It tells us, for example, that that level of household production can be had either with 30 percent of the capital and 60 percent of the labor (point P), or with 50 percent of the capital and 50 percent of the labor (point A) or with 23 percent of the capital and 73 percent of the labor (point P′).

The slope of an isoquant tells us how much of one input (say labor) has to be added to prevent any reduction in the level of output when one unit of the other factor (say capital) is transferred to production in the other sector. In a real sense, this is the *cost* of a unit of labor. It tells how much capital a unit of labor is worth in those circumstances.

If units of labor and capital sell for a money price, or wage, the households and firms will make the most of their opportunities if they adjust their use of labor and capital until the amount added (or lost) to physical output by small changes in the quantities of labor and capital is exactly proportional to the price, or wage, that they must pay for them. Another way to say this is that at the optimal position the last dollar spent for labor increases output just as much, but no more, than the last dollar spent for capital.

If, after this has been done, it is found that the price paid for labor in both sectors is the same, and the price paid for capital is also the same in both sectors, there will be no way to produce that combination of outputs with a smaller amount of labor and capital. All points on line HPM meet this requirement. All points not on HPM do not.

Points on line HPM meet this requirement because the isoquants for the two sectors are tangent on HPM. Tangency implies adjustment to the same prices, or at least to the same ratio of labor to capital prices. The common price ratio is illustrated by the dashed straight line which is tangent to hh′ and to mm′ at P. Some additional explanation is helpful.

It is important to remember that one goes from lower to higher amount of household production as one proceeds from M toward H, and that one goes from lower to higher amounts of market production as one proceeds in the opposite direction on the same curve. If we are on line MPH say at point P, there is no way to increase the amount of market produced goods, M, without reducing the supply of household produced goods and leisure. This is the significance of the tangency between the isoquants for household goods, such as hh′, and for market goods, such as mm′.

If we are at any point away from line HPM more can be produced of both household and market goods with the same amount of resources. Suppose, for example, that we are at point P′. It is on the same isoquant for household goods as P, so the same amount of household goods (and leisure) will exist as before. But the isoquant for market produced goods is lower than the one that goes through point P. It is the same as at point B on the line of optima. It follows that any reallocation of resources shown by the short line (or "contract curve"), BP, will result in a larger output of both goods.

Notice that the slopes of the isoquants $m_2m_2′$ and hh′ at point P′ are very different. The household sector is finding labor cheap relative to capital, and so is using too much labor and too little capital. The situation is reversed in the market sector.

The principal argument of this book is that labor costs which are too high to employers, account for a strong tendency of modern economies toward nonoptimal equilibria like point P′.

Other explanations exist. It may be helpful to digress briefly and comment on two conditions that could make the cost of labor high as compared to the cost of capital in the market sector. The most obvious explanation, and also the most unlikely when the *total* supply of labor is considered, is that labor union monopoly drives wages above the competitive level in the whole market sector. This is unlikely when labor as a whole is considered because no means exists to monopolize labor as a whole. Monopolies over portions of the labor market result in the use of less labor of particular types, with the "surplus" being forced to compete for the other jobs. This drives wages down elsewhere. The net effect is not likely to affect the average wage rate much. Although this is true, it is also true that the effect of monopolies in some portions of the labor market misallocate some labor, especially among firms in the market sector.[a]

---

[a] It is quite possible, on the other hand, for a totalitarian nation to hold wages *below* the competitive level in the market sector. Where a national government prohibits

In chapter 4 it was conceded that Keynes' analysis of capital goods prices relative to labor costs could be correct. To be adequate, Keynes' analysis must show that capital goods costs to the market sector are low when compared to capital goods costs in the household sector, in the absence of corrective actions. The critical matter is the *ratio* of input prices. This case can, I think, be made up to a point. Economies of scale both in physical productivity and in the financial markets are important advantages that accrue primarily to the market sector. Nevertheless, the case is overstated when it is said that "asset prices are wrong and it is to asset markets that the cure, if possible, should be applied." Attempts to achieve full employment by Keynesian means, produce inflation. This can be avoided if labor costs to employers are brought into line with social costs.

Analysis of "Unemployment"

The present analysis can be used to analyze the matter of optimal employment. Unlike Keynesian analysis, production and employment in the household is recognized. But we do agree that optimal employment and output requires more activity in the market sector than will occur under modern conditions.

The total hours available (labor force times twenty-four hours per day) are measured along the vertical axes of panel A, figure 4–1. It includes

---

private enterprise by holding nearly all productive assets in its own hands, it attains monopoly power over wages offered in the labor market. This power may be supplemented by severe restrictions on emigration, and heavy taxation of such small-scale private and cooperative enterprises as are permitted to exist. Such power makes it possible to attract long hours of work from its populace in return for lower rewards in the form of consumer goods than would result if each producing unit had to compete with the others to attract workers. Wages can be set low enough to virtually force all adults to work. Consumer goods, such as housing, can be allocated on bases that encourage work. Wage incentive systems that penalize small outputs and pay a bonus for large outputs can induce more work for less total pay. No employer will be able to attract a superior labor force by offering a better deal, because no other employer is permitted to exist.

Such a system may indeed be optimal from the viewpoint of those who hold the totalitarian power in their hands. It is not uncommon for economists, especially development economists, to find merit in such arrangements. It permits a more rapid expansion of capital goods creation (or military power) than would be possible if firms were directed to the satisfaction of the wants of the many individuals in the nation who were left free to choose from a variety of competing employers how much they wished to work and to choose among a wider variety of goods produced by the competing firms. Those in charge of production which is not monopolized by the state must produce goods that the consumers prefer (rather than those the planners want) in order to meet their expenses of production.

Those who laud "totalitarian efficiency" have preferences closer to the planner's and do not find much merit in attempting to please the general run of the population. Economic theory is typically based on the democratic, rather than the elitist view of what is optimum. From that point of view, totalitarian underpricing of labor is also inefficient, failing to optimize because it requires too much work. Point D in figure 4A–1, which represents underpricing of labor in the market sector, is exactly as inefficient as P'. More goods are produced at point D but there is less satisfaction than at point P.

the total number of potential hours of work and also the hours not worked. The hours not worked are often called "leisure." "Leisure" is a misnomer for many of the hours not worked in the market sector. As already noted, considerable time is spent in household production for home consumption. Food preparation, housework, repairs, yardwork, dressmaking, and the like could all be purchased, but are performed in very large quantities in the nonmoney economy. If the analysis of this appendix is correct, the mispricing of labor results in too much of those sorts of work being performed in the household sector. It is not right to say that people not employed in the money sector are unemployed, but most of them are not efficiently employed.

The U.S. government's statistical definition of an unemployed person requires the person to be able to work, willing to work, actively seeking work, and without a job in the *market* sector. All four conditions must be met.

No system for harmonizing factor prices should fully eliminate unemployment thus defined. There will always be someone looking for a better job, and quitting the old one so as to look more intensively, often in some distant region. There will also be short-term layoffs needed to accommodate work to the seasons, to new technologies, to changed resource availability, to shifts in consumer preferences, and to other changes in conditions. But these changes will come much closer to amounting to a simple choice between work and leisure if each adult is given the choices that are suggested in chapter 5. The personal costs involved in "actively seeking work" will be drastically reduced. In large part this is a natural consequence of having a concrete way to show willingness to work. Likewise the pressure to urgently seek a job in order to maintain a regular flow of income will be reduced.

Either "unemployment" or a "slave society" exists when there is a departure from the preferred division of potential labor hours among work in the market sector, work in the household sector and the time desired for sleeping, eating, and leisure activity. Unemployment exists when individuals have to spend more time in household production and leisure than they want to in view of the relative gains to them of additional work at current wages in the market sector as compared to the satisfactions that they can obtain for themselves in the household sector. A slave society exists when individuals must work more hours in the market sector than they would prefer when they compare their apparent alternatives.

When society tends to an equilibrium like P′ the typical worker will feel a desire to work more hours. He will value his job and work hard at it. He will spend time and effort searching for better opportunities. But the situation for employers is such that the demand for labor will be rather weak.

When society is at a point like D, the typical worker will feel that work is overabundant, that he is being pressured to work more than he wishes to. Jobs will not be highly valued. External discipline will be "necessary." Turnover rates and absenteeism will be high, and labor will be used wastefully. Nevertheless, from the point of view of the planners, "unemployment" will exist despite official statements to the contrary. They will regard many who are able to work but unwilling to work as "unemployed."

The amount of unemployed manpower cannot be measured unambiguously in figure 4A–1, but it is indicated by the difference between the 27 percent of labor hours employed in the market sector when factor price ratios do not reflect social costs, and the 40 percent employed there when they do. We take this as an index of the amount of unemployment. Unemployment is some fraction of the 13 percent of labor time misallocated to the household sector when factor prices, as illustrated here, are not optimal.

Translation to Outputs

It is awkward to compare the output of the two sectors taken together with each combination of inputs if one must read off the two outputs from numbers attached to the different isoquants. Professor Johnson's article shows how the comparison of outputs can be clarified if a quite reasonable, and often used, assumption is introduced.

The assumption is that if both factors of production are increased (or decreased) in strict proportion, the output will change in the same proportion. The change of inputs in strict proportion for both goods is shown by the straight line HM in panel A.[b] A movement down the line from H toward M takes a given proportion of the labor and capital stocks from the household sector and transfers them to the market sector.

If the assumption that output increases in proportion holds, we can represent the increase in output as a proportion of the increase of *either* labor or capital. Our figure shows the output of the market sector as proportional to the amount of labor used in that sector, and the output of the household sector as proportional to the amount of capital devoted to it. This makes it possible to draw panel B which shows the largest possible ranges of output under three conditions. The straight line H'A'M' in panel B shows all possible combinations of outputs (the "production possibilities") if labor and capital are in fact used in the same proportions in both industries. It corresponds to line HAM in panel A. Line H'Q'M' in panel B illustrates the production possibilities when private costs of inputs depart from their social costs, and corresponds to line HP'P''M in panel A. Line H'Q₀QM' in panel B illustrates the highest attainable production possibility curve where the private cost of each input coincides with its social cost. It corresponds to curve HBPM in panel A.

The optimal line, like HBPM (panel A) curves away from the straight line HAM when one good is more "capital-intensive," or less "labor-intensive," than the other. We assume that the household sector is relatively more labor-intensive than the market sector because this is consistent with the hypothesis that labor is overused in the household sector as a consequence of its being relatively cheap there.

The relationship between input combinations and output combinations

---

b Technically, the "production function" is "linear of degree one."

is explained in terms of just two pairs of points, an optimal pair P (in Panel A) and Q (in Panel B); and a sub-optimal pair, P' and Q'. Consider point P first. It is optimal for reasons already given since isoquants hh' and mm' are tangent to each other there. It is not possible to increase the output of one without reducing the output of the other.

The total output of household goods is the same at every point along the hh' curve, including the point where it crosses the straight HM line, at point A. If labor and capital were used in the 50-50 proportion shown at point A total output would be a certain amount, a given proportion of the quantity of *either* labor or capital. We use the proportion of output of household-produced goods to capital assets used in the households and assume the proportion to be 1:1. The guideline immediately above panel A, and to the left of panel B shows the 1:1 relationship. Thus the output of household goods is given by 50, as shown in the vertical axis of panel B.

The ratio of input to output in the market sector is assumed to be 1:1½. If point A actually designated the amount of labor and capital used in both output sectors, the indifference curve for market goods would be the dashed line passing through point A. In that case, the quantity of market goods produced would be 1½ times the labor used in the market sector, or 50 times 1½ or 75, as is shown on the horizontal axis of panel B.

Resources are used much more efficiently when combined in the proportions shown by point P. The higher indifference curve mm' is relevant to that point, and the equivalent output is that associated with point C on the HM curve. This is associated with a capital use of 60, and since the output of goods and services in the market sector is 1½ times that, output in the market sector is 90, as shown on the horizontal scale of panel B.

Extending the lines upward from 90, and rightward from 50 we determine point Q. It shows that with inputs divided as shown by point P in panel A, we obtain the output Q as shown in panel B. This is better than point A because more market goods and the same amount of household goods are produced with the same amount of resources.

If all of the labor and capital are devoted to household production, total output is 100 of household goods and none of the market goods. Likewise if all resources are devoted to market goods, 150 of them and none of household goods would be produced. Thus we have three points. The curve $H'Q_0QM'$ is a smooth line drawn through them. It lies well above the straight line H'A'M'.

Nonoptimal factor pricing produces the intermediate production possibility curve H'Q'M'. It is derived in exactly the same way using the isoquants that pass through point P' in the input market. The output combination Q' is the natural result of factor prices that differ between the two sectors so as to induce input combination P'.

A Welfare Function

It is now possible to take the second step toward finding the point in the Edgeworth Box that "best satisfies human wants." I should reiterate that this carries the argument beyond the main purpose of this book. It is evident that the point must lie somewhere on the optimal line HBPM in panel A, which is equivalent to H'Q$_0$QM' in panel B. Every point on H'Q$_0$QM' is "more efficient" than any on H'Q'M' or H'A'M' (except at points H' and M' where the lines converge).

The problem of finding the output that best satisfies the wants of the millions of individuals even in a single nation is most difficult. The individuals have competing needs and interests, make differing contributions to output, and have differing amounts of influence which rest on different bases. Nevertheless, some things are clear. Positive amounts of output of many different things are desired. This means that as more of something is acquired, lesser values are served by additional amounts. It is quite possible to have too much food, and too little beauty even if in times of great deprivation one would sell the most valuable art object to obtain a low quality ration of food. It follows that the best output combination is one which involves some production of many things. Diagrammatically this consideration gives the welfare, or "social indifference" curves the generally convex to origin shape that is illustrated by the WW curves in panel B. This makes it virtually certain that there will be only one "best" combination of outputs.

At the optimal point, Q$_0$, the prices of the market goods, and of the household-produced goods (and of leisure, implied by the slope of the W-curve) are exactly equal to cost to the individual of obtaining the income it takes to acquire them. The cost of acquiring the goods to each individual is affected by his income from wealth and welfare payments, and by his personal income earning ability. The optimal point, illustrated by point Q$_0$, accepts these differences. Note that the optimum is found after each individual's position has been adjusted by welfare and other income and opportunity redistribution programs.

The three social indifference curves shown are part of a "welfare function" which shows what the preferences are for every possible output. Every point on any particular indifference curve is exactly as satisfactory as any other point on the same indifference curve. For example, social wants are satisfied equally well at points Q' and E. (Perhaps we have drawn the curves too nearly flat in your opinion. It is not possible to know how flat they really are.) Social indifference curve W$_B$ is the highest attainable with factor pricing that gives us line HP'M (Panel A) and H'Q'M' (Panel B). Q$_0$ can be reached only with optimal factor pricing.

Maximum Gross National Product
Is Not Optimal

Note that the efficient output combination designated by point E is not any better for the people in the nation than is the inefficient point Q'. It is worse than the inefficient point F. In a broader sense, therefore, if "inefficiency" is defined in terms of satisfying people's wants, it is not enough to produce with technical efficiency. It is equally important that the things produced be the things preferred by the people to the other possibilities. Planners have a strong tendency to try to attain points like E or even G rather than Q_0. Gross National Product almost completely omits the value of production in the household sector. Thus a GNP of 120 (point G) can look more attractive to a growth-minded administration than a GNP of 85, which is the optimal level as shown by point Q_0.

It is clear from panel B that Q_0 is slightly better than Q. A small shift toward point M in panel A is needed to get the best output, Q_0. The value of a little more market-produced goods at point Q is a little lower than the value of household produced goods and leisure which require the same amount of labor and capital.

5

Policies to Equalize Private and Social Costs of Labor

The choices confronting policy-makers appear to offer a dilemma: either they continue the categorical programs that have earned a reputation for high cost, fraud, and failure to reach more than half the poor, or they ask for high tax rates on earnings of welfare-beneficiaries (or the equivalent in reduced benefits associated with earnings) to discourage application by most families. It will be recalled that high tax rates reduce work effort, leaving some not working at all who would work if the income transfer was not subject to special taxes not applied to other sources of nonwork income. Others simply work less.

Both systems perpetuate class division. If one is to get aid under the present welfare program he must be certified as incapable of work or more useful if not working. Alternatively, the welfare reform proposals discriminate against a welfare recipient by imposing a 50 percent, or higher, tax on his earnings (a burden not reached again until the $45,000 bracket, *after* deductions). This makes unduly attractive a life of underachievement and relative indolence. Neither system treats the welfare recipient equally with other citizens.

Outflanking the Dilemma:
A Positive Proposal

The dilemma is apparent, not real. It seems real as long as income transfers are viewed as welfare problems that are not intimately connected with the efficient allocation of resources. This has been the fashion among economists for several generations. John Stuart Mill, a child prodigy, great mature intellect and humanitarian, believed that matters of income distribution were not closely connected to matters of efficient allocation. Modern welfare economists continue the tradition, and in an important sense it is continued here.

Welfare economists favor "lump-sum" taxes and "lump-sum" subsidies to alter income distribution when it is desirable and possible. A lump-sum tax or subsidy is a payment that does not affect prices, wages or other costs per unit of scarce resources that can easily be wasted if over- or underused. Thus, lump-sum transfers are preferred because they interfere the least with the price ratios that facilitate the use of the best amount and the best combinations of resources to produce particular goods.

A lump-sum transfer to the poor could take the form of a simple grant, say of the type proposed by the family assistance plan. By itself it would solve no problem other than the provision of a minimum income to the families receiving grants. Administrative decisions still would have to be made as to who qualifies, and differences would remain between the private and social costs of labor.

The first difficulty can be avoided if Lady Rhys-Williams' proposal were adopted. She advocates a "demogrant" in the works cited in chapter 1. A demogrant means a payment to *all* adults, whether rich or poor. Obviously this is very costly, and some arrangements must be made to retrieve as much as is paid out. Taxation to accomplish this purpose is discussed in chapter 6. At this point we only note that a lump sum tax is preferred. This rules out reductions of benefits as an individual earns additional income from work, i.e. requires that tax effects be zero.

The lump-sum grants and taxes will not by themselves do anything to narrow the gap between the social and private costs of labor. This can be accomplished by providing for a system of contracts between the individuals and prospective employers which will greatly reduce the costs of job search and attendant employment costs to both parties and, in some cases provide some subsidy to employers. In no case should it be necessary for an individual to live on less than what he receives from the demogrant. This chapter outlines a specific proposal designed to universalize welfare and optimize employment.

Some Preliminaries

We will advocate a demogrant. The basis for the payments must be determined. American practice has been oriented toward family units, with attention given to the number of children. Many foreign nations provide family allowances specifically to provide financial assistance to families with children. Professor Lampman's highly professional and exhaustive studies of poverty leads him to support assistance of this kind.[1] One reason is his focus on the reduction of poverty while keeping the transfer of income to nonpoor at relatively modest (but still necessarily large) amounts.

This book focuses on the labor markets, and so attention rests on those who may be part of the labor force. The basis for the demogrant is, therefore, the adult person, taken here as being all those over the age of 20. A man and wife would each receive a demogrant which would not be affected by the number of children. Exemptions in the income tax, the transfer that is involved in the public school programs and child and youth programs that are not funded directly by families with children are considered to offer sufficient child allowance. The minimum income guarantee is related to the labor market, not the number of children.

Some will find it objectionable that rich bridge-playing wives would receive a demogrant. But there is little difference between paying a larger grant to a couple, and two smaller grants to the spouses. And there is some advantage in making the payments to individuals. Each person can individually use the grant in the ways described below to achieve a more nearly optimal relationship to the employed labor force.

Another preliminary has to do with the agencies that will administer the program. The Social Security Administration and the Bureau of Internal Revenue already possess most of the machinery that is required. Either could do the job, but the Bureau of Internal Revenue has some advantages because it already has information on income from all sources for nearly every person. This is helpful primarily with regard to the "welfare tax" which is proposed in chapter 6.

A Specific Program

As already stated, there is nothing in the receipt of the demogrant, taken by itself, that will bring the social and private costs of labor closer together. On the contrary, it will widen the gap. But the grant can be used in a way that will narrow the gap, possibly even to the vanishing point.

The key use of the grant to improve the labor markets is as follows: A person who is without a job can enter the labor force by designating a particular firm, or a firm that specializes in placing individuals, as the recipient of part or all of his demogrant for a particular period of time. This does not reduce the income of the job-seeker, however, because the designated firm must transfer back to him the full amount of the demogrant directed to them unless it employs him. If it does employ him, the pay and other terms are those which are mutually acceptable to the firm and to the employee, and the firm keeps the amount of demogrant allocated to the firm by the individual for the time period that was set by him. At the end of that period a new contract is established.

The demogrant provides a minimum income which is under the control of the individual. But it is also usable to enable the individual to place himself forcefully into the labor market if he thinks that he can better himself by so doing. And it is also used to finance the job search and information costs that now make labor markets more imperfect than they need to be.

It should be emphasized that the individual does not have to assign his demogrant to anyone. He can use it for living expenses, to add to other income if self-employed, save or invest it at interest, or for other purposes of his choice.

It will be used for different purposes at different stages of life. Young people can finance much of their higher educational expenses, retirees will have it as a basic part of their retirement income, struggling writers, artists, and small businessmen will have at least this much regular income.

Choices for the Firms

The firm receiving the assigned demogrant is to have three choices. First, it may employ the person on mutually acceptable terms. The individual's remuneration may or may not include his entire demogrant. The amount allocated to the firm can be changed from time to time. If optimal employment is attained, the firm will often retain part of the demogrant. This follows from the foregoing analysis of the reason for present underemployment—the mispricing of labor to the employer—which this use of the demogrant will partially or fully correct. Alternative uses of the demogrant by firms to enhance employment is discussed in greater detail in the next section.

Second, if the designated firm cannot find a way to employ the person, it must return all of the assigned portion of the demogrant to the person. There are some administrative costs involved in processing the transfer, so the firm will be under some pressure to find something useful for the person to do and to offer mutually satisfactory terms of employment.

In many cases the designated firm will not be able to employ the individual. Its third course of action is to attempt to persuade him to switch his choice to some other firm. Consortiums of firms can exchange information and offer alternatives. Firms which need labor can be expected to advertise and make their needs known to prospective workers. Competition should help keep the portion of demogrants assigned to firms at a minimum.

Expected Changes in Labor Markets

The major effects of the program just outlined can be predicted with the aid of the type of analysis developed in this book. There are three major influences to be considered: the effects on people's income opportunity, on people's preferences, and on their information and mobility costs. The effect of the method chosen to finance the plan has an important effect on the income opportunities. Nevertheless we leave the effects of financing aside until chapter 6.

Effects on Income Opportunities and
Preferred Amounts of Work

How this plan will affect the amount of work that individuals wish to perform depends upon what the plan does to the income opportunities that the individuals have, and what the individuals' preferences are. Reasons were given in chapter 2 for believing that changed income opportunities do not change the whole preference structure. Changes of income opportunities reveal and make relevant formerly irrelevant portions of their preference structures. Attention is, therefore, focused on expected responses to changes in income opportunities on the assumption that preference functions do not change.

Three types of influences will alter the income opportunity lines. There is a positive wealth effect that follows directly from the demogrant. There is a probable effect on the wage rate received by the employee as a result of the altered situation of the employers and employees, and there are the effects of whatever taxes are used to cover the demogrant system. This may consist exclusively of a negative wealth effect, or some combination of negative wealth effects and tax effects.

The most important aspect of the demogrant from the welfare point of view is that it sets a floor below which the individual will not fall. This is true because each adult always has the alternative of receiving the full demogrant income without working. *Whatever combination of work and income that one accepts, it must be at least as satisfactory to the individual as having the demogrant income and not working.* We may think of this as the "welfare floor." It may be desirable to allow something above the minimum in some cases. Particular cases, especially aid to dependent mothers, may need substantial supplements. Such matters, however, are not discussed here.

The allocation aspect of the demogrant is, from a broader point of view, more important than the establishment of a welfare minimum. If Alchian and Stigler are correct, the basic reason why labor is high-priced to employers (relative to capital costs) is to be found in information costs, broadly construed. Stigler and Alchian tend to imply that the equilibria actually reached are optimal. But the equilibrium expenditures of time and money by private individuals and firms leaves us with what is perceived as a persistent unemployment problem. The responses to this perceived unemployment problem produce wasteful efforts to obtain job security by dozens of special groups, gross interferences with efficient international trade, and what may be purposeless inflation. If so, the use of the demogrant to finance additional information and related employment costs may improve efficiency.

It is also possible that the general run of wages to regular workers is close to optimal but that for others the employee-seeking and job-finding costs, the "employment costs," are higher than the corresponding social costs. Employment costs are high, especially for low income employees whose efforts add relatively little to output, and for whom the labor turnover rate tends to be high.

Average turnover rates in American manufacturing industry are higher than most people suspect, and are surely very costly to firms. The average *monthly* rate in 1969 was 4.7 per 100 employed. Layoffs were 1.2, and quits 2.7. The quit rate alone amounts to nearly one-third of the total number employed in a year's time. New hires were 3.7 per 100 or nearly 45 percent of the employees in manufacturing in 1969. These data imply great costs, although disorganization is less than is implied by the large overall figure because a large amount of turnover is in seasonal work, and much of the movement is by a small number of workers who move frequently from job to job. Nevertheless, turnover costs are substantial and may make wage costs relatively higher than capital costs by enough to account for 3 to 5 percent overall unemployment.

There are important recruiting, initial orientation and training costs which are largely lost when a worker quits and is replaced. If firms can reduce these costs, they can be expected to favor production processes that utilize relatively more labor. This is especially true, if at the same time, some way can be devised to attract people who will be more satisfied, and thus less likely to quit or have to be laid off because they do not perform acceptably.

The individual's assignment of part of his demogrant to a firm provides both an initial display of interest that can simplify the firms' recruiting problems, and also money to cover information and employment costs. If information and employment costs account for the difference between private and social costs of labor, it is reasonable to expect that the workers will assign less and less of their demogrant to their firm after initial employment. Indeed, for many employees, whose value to their company is high, no assignment might ever be made. High turnover rates that result in significant unemployment exist primarily in occupations that pay below average incomes, and especially for the younger, the unmarried, and for some minority groups. These will be the principal beneficiaries both of the receipt of the demogrant and of the opportunity to use it in this way.

The usefulness of this device does not depend upon the validity of the information cost explanation just discussed. An adult (a recipient of a demogrant) may find himself unemployed for any reason at all. Suppose that he would prefer to work full time for a wage income of $4,800 or more, rather than live exclusively on his $2,400 demogrant. He can put himself in the labor market by assigning for example, $100 a month for a year to a specific firm, stating his willingness to work at certain kinds of jobs. The $4,800 plus the remainder of his demogrant totals $6,000. The firm is bound to return the $100 a month promptly as long as it does not place him in a suitable position. As soon as he is placed, the firm retains the $100.

At the end of the year the individual can attempt to change the terms. Since there are many firms and many employment agencies, since the individual will be worth more to the company at the end of the year and will be saving it recruiting costs if he stays, he will probably be able to reduce or eliminate the monthly $100 assignment.

The indifference curves that we inferred from the Green and Tella data suggest that a typical person feels just about as well off not working with half the money income that he would get if he worked full time. If the individual in our example is typical, he would have been just as happy to work for $4,800 as to stay idle and live on the demogrant. At $4,800 a flip of the coin could decide whether to work or not. It may be that no firm would have been willing to hire him at $4,800. At least none would have been willing to go out and recruit him, and undertake the other employment costs and also pay him $4,800. They may calculate that they would spend so much that they would net only $4,000 the first year and $4,800 the second. They might feel that the chance of his staying longer than two years is too small to justify hiring him at $4,800. So this individual will be employed only if he makes an active effort that convinces a prospective employer that he might stick. But he is not inclined to make such an effort under the conditions that exist today.

Both the employer and the individual gain from his offer of $100 paid out of his demogrant. The net cost to the employer is reduced to $3,600. This is $400 below their estimate of his value to them, the first year. If he stays with them he saves recruiting and training costs of perhaps $800 every year thereafter. The firm is more likely to hire him, and generally use somewhat more workers and somewhat less of other factors to get a given job done. The individual gains more. He retains $1,200 from the demogrant, and earns $4,800 more for a total of $6,000. He is much better off working than not working, and should be still better off in the second year when he is able to reduce the assigned demogrant by at least the employment costs that his staying saves the firm.

The net gains are not this big, since the cost of financing the demogrant is not yet accounted for. But net gains remain, as is shown in chapter 6.

A Definition of Unemployment:
Situation One

The four panels of figure 5–1 illustrate the preference curves for a person with the same income earning ability at different stages of his life. Two situations are shown; one where the demogrant is forfeited if the person works, and the other, where the individual and the firms have the choices just described. The position of the individual who loses the demogrant if he works is described first.

In each of the four panels of figure 5–1 the OI line indicates the value of his output to his enterprise. The amount of the demogrant remains the same and is designated by point D in each panel. Income from nonwork sources other than the demogrant are excluded, as are losses to a welfare tax. The line DY shows his total income from the demogrant plus wage income, but this line is relevant only to the second situation, where the demogrant is not sacrificed if one works (discussion of which is deferred to the next subsection of this chapter).

Three levels of satisfaction are indicated in each panel. It happens that two of them coincide in panels B and D. The indifference curve designated AA' is the highest attainable by the individual if he receives a demogrant. It, like income line DY, is relevant only to the second situation. DD' is the indifference curve which reveals the level of satisfaction equal to living on the demogrant and not working. O'O'' is the indifference curve that shows the level of satisfaction when one lives from the income from work alone, i.e., without a demogrant. Consider situation one, curves OI, O'O'', and DD' only.

A given individual during a lifetime under the conditions of the first situation is likely to pass twice through the three economic stages illustrated by panels B, C, and D. He begins and ends not in the labor force (panel D) is unemployed (in a sense to be defined shortly) early and late in his career (panel C), and is a marginal worker briefly in his youth and in his maturity. Panel A represents the prime working ages, where the person has both health and responsibilities. This is shown by the location of his O'O''

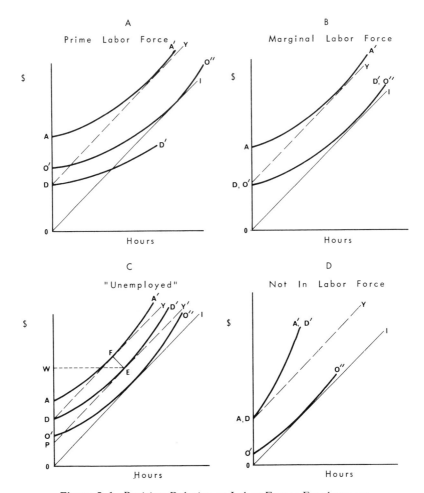

Figure 5-1. Position Relative to Labor Force: Employment.

curve, above his DD' curve. This tells us that he would rather work than live on his demogrant. On either side of the prime age one is likely to pass through a period where he is a marginal worker, that is, where, with welfare support available if he does not work, working is just barely (or not quite) worth the effort. This is illustrated in panel B where the O'O" curve coincides with the DD' curve. At any moment there is a 50–50 chance that he will be employed. Those who provide him with welfare income, however, are likely to think that he should support himself.

The person whose situation is described by panel C will be "unemployed" if he can have nonwork income equal to D. Diagrammatically, this is shown by the location of his DD' curve above his O'O" curve. He is not working under these conditions because he has too little need for money, because he has few responsibilities, or perhaps because he is disabled, making work too painful to be worth the gain. In each case, the private cost of locating suitable employment is high enough to lead him to prefer to live on the demogrant. He may be able to work, willing to work, and actively seeking work. But he is not quite able enough, willing enough, and active enough to find it, at least not promptly. Still, he would prefer work if the taxpayer did not reduce the demogrant if he worked. We define a person in this position to be unemployed. It is stated in terms of individual preferences and the discrepancy between private and social costs.

The foregoing definition is stated in terms of a demogrant. But it applies whenever a person can count on the support of others if he does not work. This is characteristic of modern societies.

Panel D remains to be described. It is primarily useful for the second situation because it provides a basis for a definition of the optimal size of labor force. In panel D the levels of satisfaction AA′ and DD′ coincide and are as steep or steeper than the dashed line DY at the axis. Recall that curve AA′ describes the highest level of satisfaction attainable if one can work without sacrificing any part of his demogrant. The person's preferences shown in panel D are such that he will not wish to work even if he did not have to sacrifice any part of his demogrant. Such a person finds even the first hour's work too costly to him to be worth the gain. The optimal amount of work, both for him and for the others who support him, is no work at all. It will not pay the others to induce him to work. Therefore, he is not in the optimal labor force.

Situation Two

All of the individuals whose positions are illustrated by panels A, B and C are in the optimal labor force if they may use the demogrant provided by the others in their society (and very negligibly by themselves) in the way described in this chapter. This is obvious at a glance because in each case the person gets to a higher indifference curve, AA′, tangent to the higher income line, DY. Only the person who is not in an optimal labor force is unaffected by a change from situation one opportunity to situation two opportunity, as we just discovered when panel D was analyzed. Except for those outside of the labor force, each person can attain some work which is better for both the individual and for those who provide the demogrant.

This conclusion was already reached in the previous example of the man who wanted a minimum $4,800 income and got $6,000. (He is like a person in panel B.) But it is well to go through the argument again using a panel C person.

The person in panel C is at point D on the indifference curve DD′ if he can have the demogrant only if he does not work, or if his benefits are reduced for each dollar earned. He would be worse off to work for what the firm can offer—a wage that produces income possibility line OI. He can work and attain point F on the income possibility line DY, and the higher indifference curve, AA′, if he can keep the whole demogrant and add to it all the wage income from the firm. That is a possibility, and it is much better than being any place on DD′. So this unemployed person may search for a job on his own and get to point F if he is lucky and finds the job without much effort. Alternatively, he may pay out any amount up to the amount DP to a prospective employer and be certain that his level of satisfaction will not fall below DD′. If he pays out DP, his total income line is depressed to PY′. But even then, the worst that he can do is to wind up at point E which leaves him working, with a money income, W, about twice the demogrant, but no better off in terms of satisfaction than at point D. Most likely he will wind up between E and F. In that case, he will be better off, and his employer will be better off also. Either way, the demogrant will have financed the costs that were keeping the man and the job apart.

Definition of "Unemployment" and "Labor Force"

Present definitions of labor force and unemployment have a high subjective content. A person is in the labor force if he is able, willing, and either actively seeking work or employed. A person is unemployed if he meets the first three criteria. Dispute exists even about the meaning of the concept "employed." Suppose a person employed two-thirds time wishes to be employed full time, or only one-third time. Is he "partly employed," or "somewhat unemployed?" We leave these questions aside.

It is much more difficult to determine whether a person is able, willing or actively seeking. Suppose he is only interested in jobs that pay $10 an hour, or $20. Suppose that the job must be in Dallas if he is to show interest. These may be reasonable demands, or they may not be, depending upon the circumstances of the individual. Is a person with a bad heart "able" or is he not? It depends upon the individual, and what kind of abilities he has. It is better to recognize that a large subjective element is unavoidably present in the definition of labor force and unemployment and define the terms accordingly.

Useful working definitions flow easily from the analysis just presented. A person is in the labor force if he is either at work or has assigned some portion (perhaps all) of his demogrant to a prospective employer. A person is unemployed if, having assigned a portion of his demogrant to a prospective employer, he remains without a position.

These definitions are straightforward, and are closely related to individual preferences and to general economic conditions. Equally important, they are closely related to a concept of optimal social costs. Those who remain either out of the labor force, or unemployed, are those who contribute most (or cost the least) as a labor reserve. They are paid a demogrant to sustain them in this status. They are not obliged to attempt to get out of the reserve. A mechanism exists which provides substantial assistance to those who wish to become employed. If they fail to get employment in any period of time, there is reason to believe that employing them would reduce the welfare of others because the cost of employing them exceeds their prospective contribution to production.

Some Additional Considerations

Several aspects of this particular scheme should be mentioned. When a person has committed an offense that results in a jail or prison term, his demogrant can be assigned by the court to the institution to which he is committed. Likewise, when a person, or his legal guardian commits a person to complete nursing home care, the demogrant can be assigned to that institution. A considerable portion, perhaps all, of the expenses of institutional care at the basic level can be covered by the demogrants. Adequacy depends upon the size of the grant, something that we defer to chapter 6 and discuss in connection with financing.

Some problems may arise because the individual may not have a good idea of the size of income that a job could bring to him. Generally, the higher the income, the more of the demogrant he would be willing to assign to get the position. There is no provision in the suggested procedure that deals with this problem. But there is some reason to hope that it is not a serious problem. If a person offers too little, he will not be employed quickly and he will get counter-offers and/or requests to switch his designated employer. If he offers more than is needed, it can still be said that he bettered himself according to his own preferences, and with experience he can hope to do still better.

There is a serious problem as long as legally-determined minimum wage scales are enforced. The same problem exists, sometimes in aggravated form, where union wage scales exist. The problem is that the productivity of the worker may not justify paying the artificially high wage rate. A second-best solution is possible if the demogrant is used by the employer to subsidize the wage. A $1,200 demogrant, for example, works out to 60¢ an hour for 2,000 hours. A youth whose contribution to output is thought to be worth only $1.00 an hour cannot be legally employed at that wage. He can, nevertheless, be paid a minimum wage of $1.60 if the demogrant is used to supplement the wage. As a result, the youth who would otherwise have the $1,200 demogrant income only, can obtain an income of $3,200 ($1.60 times 2,000 hours) plus valuable work experience that can be expected to increase his future productivity.

Comparison with the Keynesian Remedy

The Keynesian remedy attempts to harmonize the ratio between factor prices by increasing the demand for capital goods and thereby raising their prices relative to wages. The remedy presented in this chapter attempts to harmonize the factor price ratio by lowering the labor cost to the employers.

We have presented some reasons that strongly suggest that the Keynesian remedies fail to alter the ratio, or least do not alter it enough. Attempts to change it further lead to general inflation rather than changed factor price ratios.

It is possible that the fault lies in poor execution of policy rather than in the Keynesian prescriptions themselves. Suppose that that is true and that performance can be improved. Is there any reason to choose to attempt to overcome the unemployment problem by lowering labor costs to employers, rather than raising their capital costs? I believe that there are good reasons to favor the reduction of their labor costs.

The use of a demogrant to lower wage costs has some advantages which the attempt to raise capital goods costs does not have. First, it recognizes and utilizes the widespread desire for a welfare minimum of income. If emphasis is placed on expanding the demand for capital, the welfare system is placed outside of the main considerations relevant to full employment. Yet it seems clear that the nature of the welfare system and the size of the benefits provided have an important bearing on the incentives to work, and thus upon the criteria which define full employment.

More important, a program that attempts to reach optimal employment (which is a superior goal to full employment) needs to have some direct contact with the choices of individuals between work and leisure when they are not coerced by economic necessity or by administrative rules. The demogrant program does this, while the Keynesian remedies touch on these matters indirectly if at all. Thus the policy goals of government can be much more closely in touch with the preferences of the people, so that the level of employment deemed "optimal" will be closer to the mark.

There is another important consideration. Because the approach to optimal levels under the demogrant system involves actions that reduce labor costs to employers (rather than increasing their capital goods costs), it is much easier to move to the optimal level of employment at constant prices, or even falling prices. It removes the dilemma of possible inflationary price movements that may be necessary to maintain full (optimal?) employment.

Finally, this approach makes it easier to believe that optimal employment can occur without ever-growing production and resource use. A mechanism will exist whereby the size of demogrant can provide for an adequate basic distribution of output which can produce a wealth effect that will reduce the amount of labor that people will wish to provide without interfering with the efficient use of resources. We will no longer *have* to grow in order to avoid economic distress.

Summary

This chapter has attempted to present policies consistent with the theory of unemployment drawn up in chapter 4 and its appendix that can reduce, even eliminate, unemployment.

The specific proposal advanced will reduce labor costs to employers but will reduce neither the money incomes nor the real incomes of employees. (It should increase their real incomes by improving efficiency.) The proposal calls for a generalization of the welfare system to all adults, and uses their benefits (demogrants) in such a way as to lower labor costs to employers. The individuals have a wide range of choice and so do the employers, public and private. The outcome should, therefore, be close to an optimum because no one would have to agree to anything worse than what they could enjoy from the demogrant income without working. At the same time the size of the labor force and of output should increase.

Chapter 6 continues the discussion, by attempting to determine the optimal levels of the demogrant, and the optimal manner of financing.

Size of Welfare Payments and Financing

Two critically important matters are deferred in chapter 5—the appropriate size of the minimum income, and the sources of revenue to finance the program. Each is examined here.

Size of Demogrant

There probably is some optimal size for the demogrant. But until there is a rather good understanding of the consequences of alternative sizes of the demogrant upon production, employment, and other important matters, one cannot make an intelligent estimate of the optimal size. Nevertheless, something can be said about upper and lower bounds within which the optimum probably exists.

During the years 1969–71 the pressures of the political process moved Congress strongly toward a minimum income of $2,400 a year for a normal family with two children. The National Welfare Rights Organization campaigned for a $6,500 minimum. The amounts provided by contemporary programs for welfare families differed greatly from state to state, and are difficult to put entirely in money terms because of subsidized housing, food stamps, coupons good for medical services and other types of nonmoney income that add to the real income of welfare recipients. It is certain that many states provided welfare families with more than twice the proposed $2,400 minimum.

In the last analysis, the size of a guaranteed minimum income reflects two basic conditions; first, the amount those who are producing the income wish to transfer to the others, and second, the amount they are able to transfer. The latter, of course, can be expected to affect the former significantly. A welfare program that reduces total production will reduce both the ability and inclination to maintain the real income of those on welfare. Chapter 4 shows why this real danger is contained in the Nixon and especially the National Welfare Rights proposals. An optimal system should increase total production. The remainder of this chapter proceeds on the assumption that total production of the market sector is unchanged.

Some insight into the possible size of a demogrant may be sensed by considering the capitalized value of a guaranteed $2,400 family income, the size proposed by the Family Assistance Plan in 1971. A 5 percent return on an investment costing $48,000 yields $2,400. Thus a guarantee of $2,400 a year is like the gift of $48,000 with the proviso that the capital is not to be reduced. A demogrant of approximately the same size would

113

involve $1,000 a year to each adult, with no provision for children in the demogrant program itself.

There were 125 million individual Americans over twenty years of age in 1969, whom we shall define as adults. If each were given a $1,000 demogrant, the gross cost is clearly $125 billion, almost as much as the sum of public and private health, education and welfare transfers in 1967. Capitalized at 5 percent, this implies a capital value of $2,500 billion or $20,000 per adult. Higher rates of interest would yield lower values, for example, an 8 percent rate implies a total capital value of $1,561.1 billion.

These figures can be compared to the estimated value of the capital stock of the United States. Such estimates are rough at best, but they do give orders of magnitude. The preliminary figures of 1967 show a capital stock in 1967 dollars of $2,828 billion, or $13,854 per capita, or about $22,625 per adult.[1]

It is important to realize that 41.8 percent of the estimated value of the capital stock is composed of residential construction (25.5 percent), consumer durables (11.5 percent), and residential land (4.8 percent).[a] Residences, residential land, and most consumer durables (notably automobiles) are most generally put to personal use by their owners, and produce no money income.

It is evident from the above that even a $1,000 demogrant cannot be supported by taxes placed on capital assets. An effort to do so would drive the value of assets down, possibly to zero. A confiscatory level of taxation like this would dry up investment and greatly reduce employment. The output of goods and services would drop drastically.[b]

The data just presented should not discourage those who would like to see a guaranteed minimum income more generous than $1,000 per adult. They do make clear the fact that a modern welfare program cannot be maintained without tapping income from the wages and salaries. Very large transfers from wages and salaries are already made.

Professor Lampman estimates that the poor receive something in the order of 57 percent of the public funds, exclusive of education, which are devoted to health, education, and welfare.[2] The remaining 43 percent goes to those above the poverty level. The 57 percent is about 8.2 percent of consumption expenditures. A $1,000 demogrant would have required transfers of 22.6 percent, or 2.8 times the 1967 transfer to the poor.

The 22.6 percent should not be compared directly to the 8.2 percent because the comparison grossly exaggerates the size of the increase involved. This is true because a demogrant is not a *net* transfer. Every adult receives

---

[a] The general reader may be interested to know that net foreign assets account for only 1.9 percent of the total. Net foreign assets is the value of assets in foreign nations which are owned by Americans minus the holdings of foreigners of assets located in the United States. Owners include both private citizens and governmental units in both cases.

[b] A harbinger of the effect of confiscatory policies is found in New York City where rent controls and related legislation make abandonment of tens of thousands of housing units the least lossful thing for owners despite a "housing shortage."

one, including those who pay taxes to finance it. The net transfer may be no more than the present 8.2 percent depending on how the demogrant is financed. One can question the wisdom of the enormous transfers back and forth, but we will find strong reasons to favor them in the next section.

What can be said about the size of the demogrant or minimum income that "should" be established for the United States? We must say that we do not know how to discover any purely logical maximum or minimum level. But we can also say that the analysis presented in chapters 3 and 4 shows a need for a substantial amount if it is used to close the gap between the private and social costs of labor relative to other factors of production. A "sizable" amount would seem to preclude sums smaller than $1,000 per year—$19.23 a week, an amount already considered to be too small a welfare minimum in many states.

In the remainder of this chapter we take $1,000 annually as the lower bound. $2,500 annually per adult is taken as an upper bound. The latter is an estimate of the real income of an average adult in the Soviet Union including the value of the social services provided without direct payment. A demogrant of this size would place the poorest person in the United States on a higher level than the majority in the USSR.

Financing the Demogrant

Reliable receipt of a demogrant gives each individual substantial basic security throughout his adult life. Provision of such security provides a basis for a tax to finance the grants. The specific size of the tax used here for illustrative purposes will raise enough to finance the grants even if the unexpected happens and money national income falls somewhat.

There are two major problems which must be overcome if a demogrant is to work efficiently. The overwhelming majority of the voting public, not just the net recipients of the system, must think of it as being fair. The system must, at the very least, not impair productive activity. It should in fact improve productivity.

If it is not to impair productivity in the more fundamental sense, it is important that the taxes that finance the plan not greatly disturb the relationship between the amount that is added to the value of output by additional work, (the "marginal value" of work to others), and the amount that is added to the income of the worker (his "marginal income") when he performs additional work. Only then will the individual be inclined to work an optimal amount, and be able to divide his time rationally between leisure, household work, and work for money income.

There are taxes that do not change marginal values. Basically, they are lump sum taxes. Examples are licenses, poll taxes, and property taxes— taxes that must be paid if one is to engage in the licensed activity, vote, or retain possession of his property. But they collect the same amount of money whether one uses his property more or less intensively.

It is always hard to find a satisfactory logical basis for taxes that are used to finance activities that benefit different individuals in different amounts and which are conceded to be beyond hope of accurate measurement. Welfare presents an even greater difficulty because it is expected that some will be persistent beneficiaries, and others will be persistent taxpayers supporting them.

Formal analysis proceeds on the observation that many on the taxpaying side *want* to give support to those either incapable of earning what the donors regard as a "decent" income, or incapable of doing so if they discharge their other social duties, such as the raising of their children to be useful members of society.[c] Formal analysis also suggests that any one potential donor is likely to give less than he would if he were assured that others did their share in supporting those in need. It is for this reason that it is more acceptable to most potential donors if funding comes from compulsory collections (taxes) rather than voluntary contributions.[3]

The relative desirability of compulsory funding leaves the form of taxation entirely open. The funding presently used differs greatly from program to program and state to state. Old Age and Survivors Insurance is funded by contributions from employees and employers, in very inexact approximation to the benefits that will eventually be received. A considerable part of unemployment compensation is funded by employers. In many states, "experience rating" adjusts the tax according to the amount of unemployment attributed to the particular business. Since all such costs are covered by the price paid by consumers, both employer and employee taxes tend to make retirement costs and unemployment costs part of the costs of production, and adjustments are made throughout the economy as a consequence of these costs. Public assistance is financed primarily by state governments. Some rely on income taxes, others on sales taxes, on property taxes, or on some combination of the three plus miscellaneous additional taxes.

The Family Assistance Plan presented by President Nixon in 1969, and modified by Congress, incorporates an implied "welfare tax." The implied tax is expected to cover a considerable portion of the cost of the program, but will leave an estimated $5 billion to be covered by other unspecified revenues of the federal government. Personal and corporate income taxes and inflationary financing will cover most of the $5 billion. The implied tax is the recapture of the initial minimum income. It takes the form of a reduction of individual grants keyed to the amount of income earned. As noted in chapter 3, the effective tax rate in the Nixon proposal was 50 percent. The version before the Finance Committee of the Senate in August, 1971 sets the rate at 67 percent. Both offer strong incentive to work less.

Some advocate higher income tax rates in place of such heavy pay-back charges. This would reduce the incentive not to work for low income families. There are additional advantages, but also important disadvantages, for an economic point of view. Its principal advantage is that it is seen as conforming to the ability-to-pay principal. It is considered right that in-

---

c Zeckhauser, "Optimal Mechanisms," is one example of this approach.

dividuals should contribute an increasing proportion of their income as it gets larger, once adjustment for the number of their dependents and other special costs have been made. This is an important plus, and any welfare tax should collect more money from those with higher incomes.

Nevertheless, use of the personal income tax to finance welfare is not desirable. A political objection is that the personal income tax finances many activities of government. When welfare costs are lumped together with other costs of government, the taxpayer has, at best, a very vague concept of how much goes to welfare. I believe that this has resulted in an exaggerated estimate and has contributed to social division.

An economic objection is that its progressive rates materially affect the slope of the income opportunity lines of those earning above average income.[d] This means that the more productive members of society (those who earn higher incomes) get to keep only a small portion of additional earnings once they have reached a moderately high income level. This discourages additional output. A tax that collects the same amount from these individuals, but does not reduce amount that the person keeps from *additional* work, would secure a higher intensity of work from the most productive members of society. The lump-sum tax does this.

The lump-sum tax can be viewed as a property tax. As such it taxes the value of a person's "human capital" in much the same way the ordinary property tax taxes the value of real properties. I believe that such a tax is eminently fair when applied to labor income.

A property tax is properly levied against "human capital" because the income earning ability of an individual is basically a return to the valuable asset that human talent is. An exact analogy exists between the value of a nonhuman asset and its income earning ability.

What determines the value of a person's human capital? Certainly much of it is not due to the specific efforts of the individual. Rather, it is the result of what he has received in his genetic inheritance, the psychological and financial support of his family, the quantity and quality of his education, the opportunities encountered for personal development, and the encouragement to take advantage of them. These can be viewed as investments incorporated in his person, many of which are not the result of his own efforts

---

[d] This characteristic is questioned by some economists. One standard view is that the amount of effort is not reduced because additional effort yields *something* more. The weakness of this argument is obvious from the analysis of chapter 3. Another view is based on the observation that people paying high marginal tax rates under our present income tax nevertheless work long and hard hours. What is relevant, however, is hours worked per lifetime. I believe that the investigation is yet to be made that will inform us about vacation time, early semi- or full retirement and similar relevant matters. In any case, what is needed at this moment is *additional* tax sources. It may follow that nothing is to be gained by making the current tax structure more progressive than it already is.

A final observation should be made. To the extent that incomes earned reflect true opportunity costs differential taxes will, over time, affect the relative supplies of labor for different types of work. This will alter pretax incomes in such a way as to tend to reestablish posttax differentials. If this is true less adjustment is required if the changes are proportional to begin with.

and sacrifices, and much of which is the consequence of tax-based expenditures.

The ability to earn an income is also very much dependent upon the continuing protection provided by government. It secures the person in the use of his personal property (which includes his own labor). It provides laws governing and protecting the contracts that he makes with others (including labor contracts) which are vitally important to his welfare. It is important to remember that our basic law gives each individual property rights in his own labor. These rights are meaningful because a person in our society can seek work from tens of thousands of independent employers, or can go into business for himself.

The value of the human capital under the control of an individual is, therefore, to a very large extent the creature of the society of which he is a part, and it is reasonable indeed that he be called upon to bear the expenses of the government of that society through taxes that are based upon the value of the properties that the individual holds.

It is at least as reasonable that the wealth incorporated in a person be taxed as it is that wealth in nonhuman form be taxed.

The principle may be clear but there are difficulties in application. The value of wealth is revealed by the income stream that it produces. Thus the form of a tax on capital must be related somehow to its income stream. There is no problem when the assets are earning assets that are bought and sold on a market. The market value of assets is kept very close to the expected values of their income streams by the market process. There is no market for human assets, since in the absence of slavery one can neither legally buy another person, nor sell himself or another person.

The direct way whereby one may estimate the value of the human capital that a person embodies is to estimate the maximum value of the outputs that he can contribute over his lifetime, and discount them at some rate of interest to their present worth. Stated this way the assessment of human capital for tax purposes is preposterous.

What can be done is to tax current income from all sources (human and nonhuman) in a way that closely approximates the effects of a property tax. Such a procedure avoids the assessment procedure while accomplishing the primary goal of avoiding incentives to work less such as are involved in the ordinary income tax. The incentive to work less is an incentive not to develop the full value of the human capital in its service to others.

The property tax, as stated before, has the effect of shifting the individual income potential line downward. It has a negative wealth effect, but no tax effect, as these terms are defined in chapter 3. This is illustrated in figure 6–1 by the parallel shift of the solid income opportunity from line OI to TT′. What is shown is the effect of the tax only; the effect of the demogrant is not shown.

Consider first the base income opportunity line OI and the welfare tax, on it. Before the tax the individual works H hours and earns Y income. An ordinary property tax affects a person's net annual income by shifting his untaxed income potential line, OI, directly downward by the amount of the

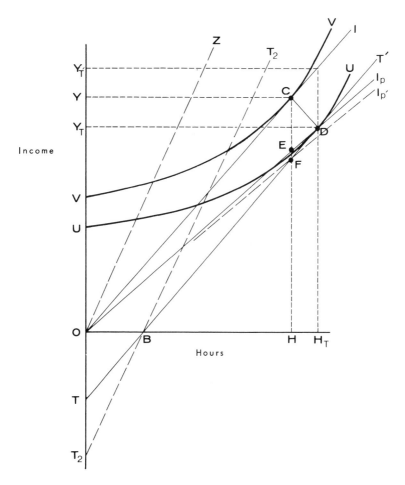

Figure 6-1. Effects of a Property-Type Welfare Tax.

tax, OT. His effective income potential line becomes TT'. Note that the tax reduces the individual's after tax income by the same amount regardless of the amount that the individual works. If he doesn't work at all his net income is the minus amount, T. Such a tax would induce an individual with the typical preference function indicated by indifference curves UU' and VV' to work H_T hours. Because more hours are worked, net income falls by only YY_T, about one-half of the tax paid. The total value of his output to society rises from OY to $OY_{T'}$.

A feasible device that has approximately the same effect as a property tax is possible. It is achieved by taxing at a 100 percent rate the *first* units of annual (or monthly) income, and not taxing any of the remainder of income earned. A tax on the first 250 hours of annual income can be graphed as the line OBDT'. In the relevant range, that is where the income possibility curve is tangent to the highest attainable indifference curve, the income potential line is identical to the one that results from a property tax.

There are difficulties involved in drawing up a tax law that will work as indicated in figure 6–1. They may be great enough to make additions to the income tax a superior choice. One disadvantage is that individuals may find ways to apply the 100 percent tax against an unrepresentative portion of their incomes. A second is that some special provision must be made to avoid discouragement of bona fide part-time workers. A third is that the tax may not be seen as a lump-sum tax. Some ways to avoid these difficulties are discussed at the appropriate places in this chapter. Superior procedures may be discovered. We examine the third difficulty first.

There is some chance that a heavy tax on the first earnings will be seen by the worker as simply a reduction of his rate of pay. This would certainly be true if the first minutes of *every* hour were taxed. At the other extreme serious problems are raised by making it the first several weeks of income out of a year. Perhaps the problem can be minimized by putting it on a monthly, or even quarterly, basis, with the tax based upon the usual number of hours or normal days worked. The tax is taken as a percentage of the normal earnings based on that number of hours or days. It is a lump sum. Actual take-home pay varies in a direct one-to-one proportion with hours worked. If overtime pay is due, it is also untaxed, since it is not earned unless the normal number of hours have already been worked.

If in spite of this kind of arrangement the worker responds as if he had simply suffered a reduction of his pay rate, he will react just as he would if the welfare tax were a strictly proportional income tax. The effect of this, and a comparison with the lump sum tax, is illustrated on figure 6–1.

A proportional income tax that imposes the same rate as the property tax illustrated when the person works H_T hours is illustrated by line OI_p. But the individual will get to the better position under this incentive system, shown by point E. At that point the person works less and pays somewhat less tax. A somewhat higher tax rate produces income opportunity line $OI_{p'}$ and collects as much money as the lump-sum tax, but induces the person to make a smaller contribution to production, as shown by point F. It will also put him on a lower level of satisfaction. Progressive income taxes have greater incentives to reduce work—and contribution to output—even as compared to a proportional income tax.

Both the property tax and the income tax provide incentive to seek better-paying jobs. A higher wage produces a higher income potential such as OZ. A normal work year of 2000 hours yields a higher return to government, OT_2, but leaves the high income earner on the higher after-tax income potential line, BT_2, as compared to BT' in the relevant ranges.

It is reasonable to tax all property in this way. Such property income as dividends, interest, and rents received can be taxed by taking a given percentage of annual receipts. In principle, the same percentage should be applied to the calculated value of owner-occupied housing and similar properties that do not yield a money income. This is desirable because the tax should not lead people to favor investment in nonhuman capital at the expense of investment in human capital—or the reverse. To do so results in the same sort of distortions that presently lead people to commit too many resources to leisure and household production.

Optimal employment can only be reached if private costs are brought into harmony with social costs. It is hard to see why we should continue to use taxes that encourage technically and economically inefficient household production and leisure when there is much poverty in the United States and elsewhere, and when such large demands exist for resources to combat pollution are needed in the market sector.

Effect of the Demogrant on the Net Welfare Tax

The stage is at last set, to consider the combined effects of a demogrant and a welfare tax sufficient to finance it. This section combines the two effects and introduces some necessary modifications.

Receipt of demogrant has a positive wealth effect that shifts the net income potential line upward. The welfare tax has a negative wealth effect that shifts the net income potential line downward. When a person chooses to assign part or all of his demogrant to a potential employer he shifts his net potential income line downward from the one that includes both the demogrant and his prospective income from labor, at least temporarily, if he is employed. If he is not employed, of course, he continues to receive the full demogrant (plus any other after-tax income from nonwork sources). The objective of the assignment—for either a presently employed or unemployed person—is to secure a position that actually yields the labor income which is only potential until a job is secured.

An attempt is made in the next section to calculate the costs of demogrants of $1000 and $2500.

The Impact of Fully Financed Demogrants on Individuals in Alternative Situations

It may be premature to attempt to construct a total program constructed from the findings presented thus far. In particular, the data problems are such as to make uncertain estimate of the cost of demogrants to individual taxpayers in different income situations. Then too, estimates of the effect of the demogrant and taxes place a heavy weight upon the preference function that we have constructed from the slender data provided by Green and Tella and corroborating evidence gleaned of other sources.

Still it is instructive to try to establish orders-of-magnitude in dollars and cents to gain perspective on the dimensions of an optimal employment problem. If one decides how large the demogrant should be, it forces attention to practical difficulties that can be fatal to an ongoing program, and it has the effect of making concrete the abstract analysis that has occupied our attention to this point. For these reasons we plunge into the icy and troubled waters of being specific.

All data are for the year 1969. I find that as I write this (August, 1971) many 1970 data are not available, and even 1969 data are often preliminary, so it is even necessary at two critical points to rely on 1968 data.

We begin by calculating annual demogrants of $1,000 per adult (all twenty years of age or more, each individually whether married or not), and follow it with calculations related to $2,500 demogrant per adult.

The One-Thousand Dollar Demogrant

In 1969 there were, as stated previously, 125 million individuals in the United States over twenty years of age.[4] A $1,000 demogrant, therefore, would have had an annual cost of $125 billion. This is, of course, a transfer and most of the 84 million in the labor force would have received the $1,000 as well as paid the welfare tax. The net transfer is very much less than the gross amount of $125 billion, perhaps not more than the $84 billion which was actually devoted to welfare (exclusive of education) in 1969.

The next task is to estimate the tax burden as a percentage of earned income. We take the sum of wages and salaries ($509.9 billion in 1969) but omit supplements and contributions to social insurance. We add to that proprietors' income ($66.3 billion), rental income of persons ($21.6 billion), net interest ($30.6 billion) and corporate dividends ($24.6 billion), but omit corporate income taxes and undistributed earnings. The total is $653 billion, approximately 70 percent of Gross National Product.

Some of the income received will not be taxed if some exemptions are made to avoid inhibiting part-time work, as suggested below. A generous estimate of the amount not taxed is the total received by families who had incomes below $4000 plus unrelated individuals with incomes below $2000. This is estimated using average income for the two groups of $3120 and $1380. The two groups earned about $40 billion. This leaves a tax base of $613 billion out of which $125 billion needs to be raised and transferred. This is 20 percent, equivalent to a 100 percent tax on the first 400 hours of work, if 50 weeks of 40 hours each is taken as the standard.

The results are described in figure 6–2 and table 6–1. Consider the figure first. The heavily drawn indifference curve labeled "minimum satisfaction" is the base indifference curve below which it is desired that no one fall. A person earning $1 per hour full time would, according to this curve, be just as satisfied to receive a $1000 demogrant (point D) as to work to get $2000. The combined effect of the $1000 demogrant and the 100 percent tax on the first 400 hours of his work puts him on the income opportunity line marked 1_N$. This is $600 above his former income possibility line. If the preference functions are as shown he will wish to work, but not enough to get $2000 in addition to the demogrant. Instead he will work enough to reach point A. His contribution to output falls about $400, his money income rises about $200 but his real income rises more by the value of the additional leisure.

The net effect of the demogrant can be read from the lower part of the vertical scale. The demogrant is $1000. The remainder after welfare tax is read by the end of the new net income opportunity line. The amount of tax

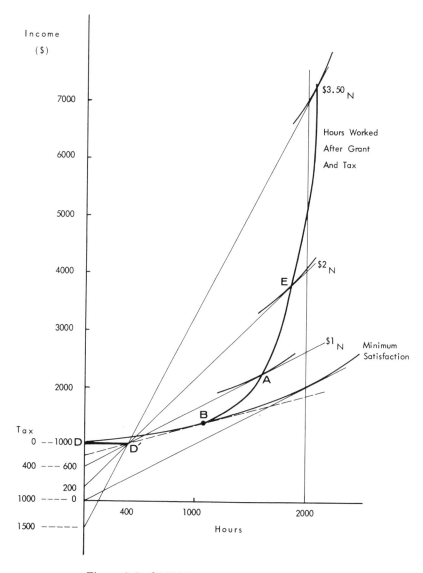

Figure 6–2. $1000 Demogrant and Welfare Tax.

Table 6-1

Estimated Costs and Benefits of
$1,000 Demogrant for Ten Income Levels: 1969

(1) Earned Income ($)	(2) Calculated Full-Time Hourly Wage ($)	(3) Demogrant ($)	(4) Welfare Tax (Days)	(5) Welfare Tax ($)	(6) Demogrant Minus Welfare Tax ($)	(7) Net Benefit as Percentage of Earned Income (%)	(8) Net Benefit Adjusted for Other Tax Savings (%)
0	0.00	1,000	0	0	+ 1,000	—	—
1,000	0.50	1,000	0[a]	0	+ 1,000	+100	+105.9
2,000	1.00	1,000	400	400	+ 600	+ 30	+ 35.9
5,000	2.50	1,000	400	1,000	0	0	+ 5.9
7,000	3.50	1,000	400	1,400	− 400	− 5	+ 0.9
10,000	5.00	1,000	400	2,000	− 1,000	− 10	− 4.1
15,000	7.50	1,000	400	3,000	− 2,000	− 13.3	− 7.4
30,000	15.00	1,000	400	6,000	− 5,000	− 16.6	− 10.7
50,000	25.00	1,000	400	10,000	− 9,000	− 18	− 12.1
100,000	50.00	1,000	400	20,000	−19,000	− 19	− 13.1

[a] Not expected to work.

can be read from the scale that starts with zero opposite 1000, and reads downwards.

A dashed income opportunity line passes through point D′. It is also tangent to the minimum satisfaction curve at point B. At a wage this low the individual will be as pleased not to work at all if he must pay a welfare tax on the first 400 hours of his work.

The somewhat steeper line marked $2 shows the net situation for a person earning that wage. The welfare tax retrieves $800 of the $1000 demogrant, leaving him $200 better off, and working a little less, as shown by point E.

The breakeven income occurs at $2.50, not shown, and beyond that point a net tax is paid. Also somewhat longer hours are worked. This is illustrated for the wage $3.50.

The combination of fixed-sized demogrant and welfare tax makes net incomes more nearly equal. The effects for ten earning rates are shown in table 6–1. The data refer to individuals who work exactly full time (50 weeks per year, forty hours a week). A series of diagrams, presented later in this chapter, illustrate the situation for three income levels. In the diagrams the hours worked are variable and so are more suitable for judging the effects of the program on incentives to work.

Table 6–1 is largely self-explanatory, but some explanation is desirable. Column 1 gives the annual income, all of which is assumed to come from current activity. Column 2 states the hourly "wage" rate on the assumption that 2,000 hours are worked annually. Column 3 is included to make certain that the reader realizes that each adult member of the labor force (along with every other adult) receives the full demogrant quite regardless of the size of his private income. Column 4 indicates the number of days per year which are subject to the welfare tax, and column 5 gives the tax in dollars. (Nonwork income is taxed at the same rate, 20 percent). If a person had work income of $5,000 and an additional $5,000 from securities, rents, etc., his welfare tax would be $2,000, just as is shown here for a work income of $10,000.

Column 6 shows the net burden on individuals in different income classes. It is column 3 minus column 5 at each level. Those with income below $5,000 receive a net benefit, those above that income pay a net tax. Column 7 shows the net benefit or tax as a percentage of base income.

The calculations presented in columns 6 and 7 do not present an accurate measure of the net cost of the tax to people at the various income levels. This is true for two reasons. They make no allowance for changed work intensity, such as that illustrated in figure 6–2. Then too, a demogrant system will replace, or greatly reduce, a number of welfare programs that are presently funded by various revenue sources. The welfare tax would replace these sources.

The impact of these revenue sources upon individuals at different income levels is largely a matter of speculation. It is not clear just who actually bears the "incidence" of the tax even when a tax is specifically levied on the employee, as in the case of part of cost for Old Age and Survivors Insurance

(OASI). This is true because it may effect wage levels and also consumer prices that affect the real income of people in income groups and locations far from the firms. Tax incidence is still less certain when the tax is placed upon the employer, as in the case of unemployment compensation, and the remainder of OASI. Other parts of the welfare program are funded from general revenues.

Studies which attempt to calculate the burden of taxes upon people at different income levels must make use of many rather arbitrary assumptions. The studies, for what they are worth, indicate that the very lowest income groups pay a large proportion of their income in taxes. Sales taxes, excises, social security and property taxes hit them relatively hard. The middle income groups are taxed somewhat more lightly as a percentage of income, but higher income groups, like the lower groups, are taxed relatively heavily due to the impact of income and estate taxes.

For our present purposes we make the assumption that the taxes that will be replaced by a welfare tax bear proportionately upon each income class. If we assume that a $1000 demogrant will replace half of the welfare program expenditures (exclusive of education) it would have reduced funding in 1969 by $40 billion. This was 5.9 percent of national income. Under the assumptions just made it reduces the net tax burden (or increases the net benefit) by 5.9 percent of income. Column 8 presents the net burden by income level after adjustment as a percentage of annual income.

Total Cost of a $1,000 Demogrant

It is not easy to talk sensibly about the total cost of a welfare program. It is essentially a system of transfers which is expected to accomplish some desired objective. Our calculations show that the cost of a $1,000 demogrant has a maximum cost to the richest person of something between 20 percent and 14.1 percent. Net benefits accrue to those with income below $5,000. Remember that these data are for individuals, not families. A family with two members each earning $4,000 would receive $200 each in net benefits. A family with one income from one adult earning $8,000 would also receive net benefits of $400, the net tax on the $8,000 being offset by the net benefit to the other.

The gross cost is high, $125 billion minus $40 billion tax saving, or about $85 billion. This is about 12.5 percent of the figure we have used for national income and is equal to the amount spent for American armed forces in the wartime year, 1969 (about 9.1 percent of the Gross National Product).

The real cost or benefit can only be assessed in terms of what it does to reduce unemployment and inflationary tendencies, what it does to reduce poverty, and what it does to further other desirable economic and social goals such as promotion of growth, reduction of pollution, and so on.

If the analysis presented in this book is correct, total national production will increase because more work is induced from most highly productive people, and by creating more opportunities for employment for many lower-middle and lower income potential individuals. Most important, individuals will have much greater personal security, making the decision between working for a money income and other activities much more a matter of choice. In this sense unemployment as a social problem will be much reduced, if not eliminated.

Effects on Incentive to Work

This section shows that the effect of the demogrant-tax program is to discourage lower income workers from working full time and encourage higher income workers to work more than full time. Three figures present the positions of three workers: one with very low income potential, one with the potential of earning the break-even income, and one with relatively high potential.

Low Income Potential

Figure 6–3 shows the choices that confront a worker capable of earning only 75 cents an hour. It is illegal for him to offer to work for that wage, or for an employer to pay a wage that low. Hence he is currently excluded from employment, even though he might be willing to work for such an income, which amounts to $1,500 a year. What will he wish to do and what can he do when his situation is changed by the introduction of a $1,000 demogrant?

His income potential line shifts up from the beginning at the origin to the parallel line that starts at $1,000. He enjoys a net wealth effect of $700 when his wage is only $0.75. It is evident that he will wish to work less than 2,000 hours, about 1500 hours, as shown by point B′ on the highest attainable indifference curve.

If the law requires payment of a $1.60 minimum wage, the income opportunity line must be at least as steep as OA′. The employer can use the demogrant (if it is assigned to him) to subsidize the wage so as to meet the minimum wage requirement. Line ADC shows the full length of the resulting income opportunity line if the welfare tax is collected on the basis of the $1.60 wage. This limits the work opportunity to about one-third of full time. Unfortunately, there is nothing that the employer can do unless the welfare tax can be reduced or the minimum wage requirement set aside.

If the welfare tax is not collected, but the minimum wage is retained, the individual's income opportunity line becomes OA′. It stops at point A′ because the full $1000 demogrant is exhausted there. The individual's preference structure shows that he would like to work more at the $1.60 wage (or, indeed at the 75¢ wage). Hence he will feel underemployed at point A′.

He is, nevertheless, better off either at point C or at A′—even assuming that he could have been employed at all prior to the demogrant-welfare tax program. And he is better off working at either C or A′ than he would be if he lived on demogrant income alone, for he will have attained an indifference curve higher than the minimum satisfaction curve.

The individual's position is worse than at B′. Marginal workers require special treatment if they are to be optimally employed in the face of rigid minimum wages.

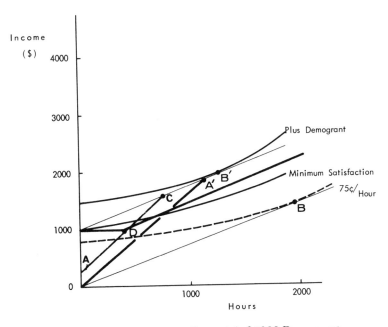

Figure 6-3. Low Income Potential: $1000 Demogrant.

Middle Income Potential

Now consider a person with higher income potential. His income is such that his welfare tax equals his demogrant. Figure 6–4 illustrates his position. The welfare tax on the first 400 hours of annual labor yields exactly $1,000, leaving the individual in the same position as before the demogrant system. His income opportunity line is altered at its lower end. Under the demogrant system it has an initial flat section at $1,000, a kink at point A, then a rising section of indefinite length going through points A and B. But the relevant range (the neighborhood of point B) is unchanged, and the amount of work that the individual will wish to perform is unchanged. He will surely wish to work, for every point on the indifference curve passing through B is very much better for him than the minimum satisfaction curve that passes through point D (where he would live on the demogrant, and not work).

If this individual were to lose his job but not his ability, assigning his

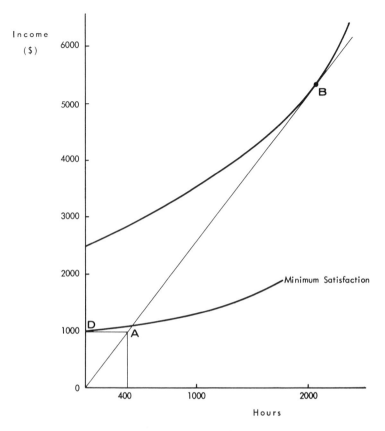

Figure 6–4. Break-Even Income: $1000 Demogrant.

demogrant in full would get him a new job quickly and at a level of satisfaction substantially above the minimum satisfaction level which is provided for by the demogrant.

High Income Potential

For the high income person we choose a person with an annual income of $50,000, his hourly wage being $25. Figure 6–5 illustrates his position. Note that the vertical scale is changed to accommodate the high income.

Under the demogrant system the "$50,000 man" finds his income opportunity line shifted from OI to DAB'I'. The welfare tax takes $10,000 of his income leaving him $9,000 poorer after receipt of the demogrant. This is a negative wealth effect which makes him work a little longer, as shown by point B'. He will wish to work 2,150 hours rather than 2,000. At $25 an hour the additional 150 hours raises his earned income $3,750. Note that

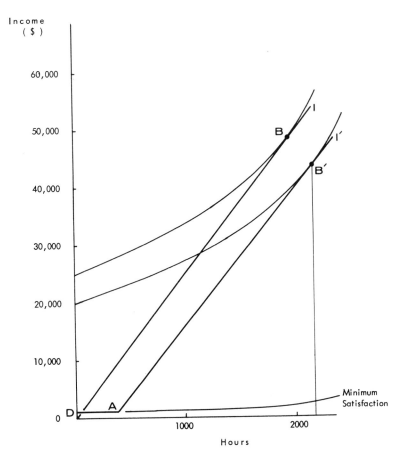

Figure 6–5. High Income: $1000 Demogrant.

none of this additional income is taxed. The demogrant system tends to induce high income people to work more.

Figure 6–5 shows the individual on a lower indifference because of the demogrant-welfare tax system. This may be a defect in the method chosen to illustrate the impact of the system. There is considerable evidence that well-to-do people *want* to provide minimum incomes for less fortunate people at some cost to themselves. If so the indifference curves shown may be somewhat misleading in spite of the fact that they correctly show the effects on work incentives. The reason for this anomaly is that individuals' desires to help others are not included in the preference curve between personal income and work that is illustrated in our diagrams. Thus it is possible that the high-income individual in some important sense prefers the lower indifference curve which is tangent to B′ to the higher one which is tangent to B when he considers the final use made of the funds taken from him by the welfare tax.[5]

It is also quite possible that the effect of the demogrant system will be to increase production and reduce serious social tensions. These results would also shift the higher income groups to higher indifference curves. No attempt is made at this point to assess these dynamic consequences.

Instead we raise a different question. What is the upper limit of the demogrant? We do not easily find a hard and fast answer to this question, but the problems encountered attempting to find a feasible way to finance a $2,500 demogrant are enlightening.

A Two-Thousand Five-Hundred Dollar Demogrant

A number of awkward problems arise when the level of the demogrant is raised to higher levels. The amount of excluded, or less than fully-taxed, income rises rapidly and the number of people who will pay a net tax declines. It becomes difficult to find ways to make sure that it is worthwhile to earn a higher rate of pay as one goes from low untaxed income to higher income levels. Nevertheless, it is possible to construct a system that would have financed a $2,500 demogrant to all over twenty years of age in 1969.

A $2,500 demogrant to each adult would have cost $312 billion. This is 47.8 percent of national income, as we have defined it. Rough calculations, like those made for the $1,000 demogrant, suggest that $115 billion of earnings are by individuals earning less than $5,000. We find a way to tax some people in these categories without causing disincentives to work, but the taxes gained will probably be fully offset by a strong tendency of others now employed part time and full time at low wages to abandon work when each adult can get $2,500, unless special provisions such as those discussed in the next section are adopted. Perhaps an average rate of tax on taxable income as high as 55 percent will suffice to cover the extraordinary cost of these transfers. This is a welfare tax on the first 1100 hours of work and income from other sources of fully-taxed individuals. I believe that this exceeds politically feasible limits and presses hard upon real, but not clearly definable, theoretical economic limits.

Table 6–2 presents data for ten levels of income which parallel the data in table 6–1. We find that individuals earning up to about $5,000 a year benefit economically, and that those earning more lose disposable income if reductions in current funding of social security programs are ignored.

It is well to remind ourselves again that the normal family is comprised of two adults. It is reasonable to expect that demogrants of this magnitude would virtually supplant existing publicly funded welfare schemes and possibly private ones as well. As a result, considerable tax-savings, and possibly other savings, will benefit all income groups. Column 7 adjusts the net benefits to reflect the elimination of public welfare expenses on the assumption that they are borne proportionally by each income class. A

Table 6-2

Estimated Costs and Benefits of a $2,500 Demogrant for Ten Income Levels: 1969

(1) Earned Income ($)	(2) Wage Rate ($)	(3) Hours Taxed (Hrs)	(4) Tax Paid ($)	(5) Demogrant Minus Tax Paid ($)	(6) Percentage of Earned Income (%)	(7) Percentage of Tax Adjusted for S. S. Tax (%)
0	0.00	0	0	+ 2500	—	—
1000	0.50	250	0[a]	+ 2500	+250	+262.5
2000	1.00	250	250	+ 2250	+112.5	+125
2500	1.25	375	469	+ 2031	+ 81.2	+ 93.7
4000	2.00	900	1800	+ 800	+ 20	+ 32.5
5000	2.50	1000	2500	0	0	+ 12.5
6000	3.00	1100	3300	− 800	− 13.3	+ 0.8
12000	6.00	1100	6600	− 4100	− 34.2	− 21.7
50000	25.00	1100	27500	−25000	− 50.0	− 37.5
100000	50.00	1100	55000	−52500	− 52.5	− 40.0

[a] Not expected to work.

substantial equalization of net income is observed. The maximum possible net tax is 42.5, with net benefits extending up to individual incomes of $6,000.

Financing is the most perplexing aspect of a $2,500 demogrant. The revenue need is enormous, and the nonwork income is high enough to offer strong disincentives to a large portion of the labor force. The solution adopted here is illustrated in figure 6–6.

The principal innovation is the introduction of a sliding scale for the tax

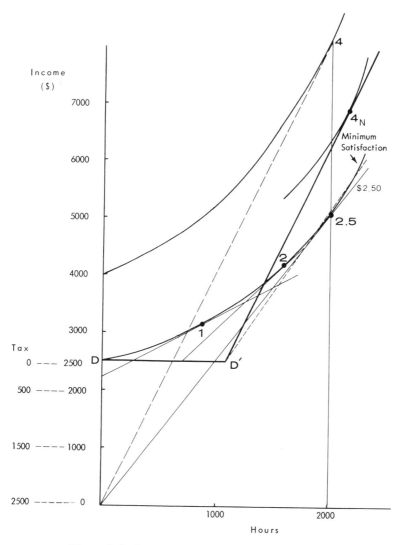

Figure 6–6. $2500 Demogrant and Welfare Tax.

base. The number of work days taxed rises from zero to a maximum of 1100 as the computed wage rate rises from zero to $2.75. This is apparently the maximum possible that will still induce those earning less than the equivalent of $2.75 an hour to work. What it does is to raise all those with a lower income potential to the indifference curve which is equivalent to $2,500 without work, the curve labelled "minimum satisfaction." The tangents to the points marked 1, 2, and 2.5 cut the DD' line at points which indicate the number of hours' work to be taxed.[e]

The shape of the minimum satisfaction curve is that tentatively deduced from the Green and Tella data and related information. It is illustrative, but is by no means accurately enough known to set the maximum taxable hours precisely. It is assumed that no one will normally work to attain an income potential which lies below the minimum satisfaction curve. If work disqualifies one for the demogrant, those capable of earning less than $2.50 an hour ($5,000 per year) will not wish to work.

Figures 6–7 and 6–8 analyze the position of two individuals with the full-time income of $2,500 ($1.25 an hour) and $20,000 ($10 an hour).

Low Income

A person with the ability to earn only $1.25 an hour can earn $2,500 income by working full time, at point A on the income potential line OA, 1.25. Every point is far below the minimum satisfaction curve which exists when he has the privilege of receiving a $2,500 demogrant. If in addition to his earnings he enjoys receipt of a $2,500 demogrant but is subject to a welfare tax as shown, he can just reach the minimum satisfaction curve at point B. Diagrammatically his choices lie on income opportunity line DD'B. A problem with the $2,500 demogrant, with its high costs, is that the worker is not perceptibly better off working, at point B, than not working, at point D. Ideally, the taxable hours should be relaxed a bit to permit him to attain a somewhat higher curve by working. If some way can be found to eliminate his welfare tax he would tend to work still less, somewhere along BB'. But if he allocates part or all of his demogrant to gain employment, a wage subsidy at the extreme might induce him to work full time at point A', even though he would be just as well off not to work.

With no demogrant system, or any other welfare (public or private), a person in this situation would work full time at point A. If the consensus of those in society is that no one should live at that low level of satisfaction, it is only reasonable that he take some of the benefit of his improved status in increased leisure. Reduced work hours are evidence that substantial progress has been made toward equilization of satisfaction among individuals.

---

[e] The rate of tax over the wage rate range $2 to $4 is awkward because the increase in net full time income is small. On the other hand, the table is somewhat misleading because the range of earned money income will differ more because low earners are expected to work fewer hours.

High Income

A person with an income greater than $6,000 pays a net tax. This places him on a lower indifference curve between work and income. Remember that he either positively wishes, or at least agrees to assist others of his society by supporting the demogrant-welfare tax program. If so, he is not on a lower point of this overall preference function, but rather is typically on a higher, or at least on no lower, plane than before. Nevertheless, his net money income is much less. Consider the effect on a person capable of earning $10 an hour—$20,000 for a normal full time year. Before the demogrant and welfare tax he would work 2,000 hours and receive a money income of $20,000, as is illustrated by point A in figure 6–7. If, after the demogrant-welfare system went into effect, he worked only 2,000 hours he would earn only $9,000 after tax. This plus his demogrant would leave him with a net income of $11,500 as in shown by point B. But since additional earnings are untaxed, he will prefer to work additional hours to attain point A′ where he will enjoy a net income of approximately $14,700.

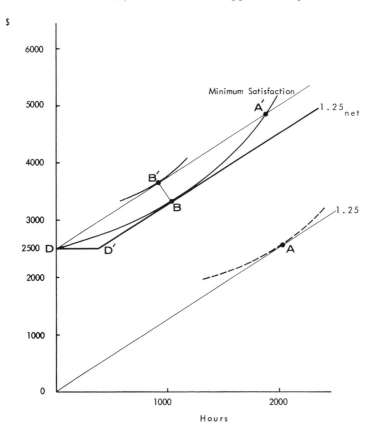

Figure 6-7. Low Income: $2500 Demogrant.

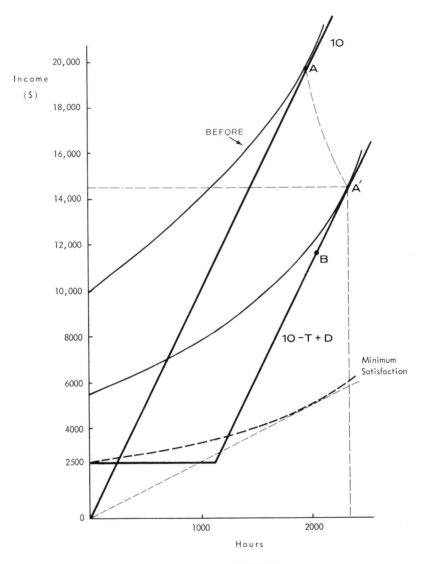

Figure 6-8. High Income: $2500 Demogrant.

This $3,200 addition to production is as much a consequence of a demogrant-welfare tax system as is the $1,500 reduction of output predicted for the person with a $1.25 wage rate. Since the dividing line is at about $3 per hour, it is quite possible that an overall increase in total output in the market sector will occur.

Equalization of Incomes

It is obvious that a demogrant-welfare tax system embraces strong equalization tendencies. Low income individuals are raised to the minimum satisfaction level or above it. Higher income individuals are brought down closer to it.

It is not so obvious, but perhaps more important, to see that the equalization is not the result of some punitive forces. It is instead the result of a discovery of ways to accomplish the social goals that people in every income group seem to have accepted. Fortunately, it is also the result of correcting input prices so as to make an optimal use of the labor force.

We can get a feeling for the amount of equalization by comparing the dollar values for the relevant indifference curves at the no-work point. Before the $2,500 demogrant welfare tax these values were $1,250, and $10,000 for the individuals shown in figures 6–7 and 6–8, respectively—a gap of 8,750. After the demogrant-welfare tax the values are $2,500 (or a little more) and $7,350—a gap of $4,850. These values show relative positions only. With the more desirable welfare system and more nearly optimal employment, the amount of satisfaction received per dollar may have increased for all.

Part-Time Workers

So far we have neglected part-time workers. Altogether they presently produce about 10 percent of total output, so it is important to understand how the system described in this chapter will affect them.

Part-time workers are defined as those who choose to work for fewer than 2,000 hours a year at wage rates suitable to their abilities.

A person may be a part-time worker because he is disabled, because household duties and other nonlabor market duties require much of his time, or because sufficient income from nonwork sources is coming in to make additional gain from added income relatively low. Hopefully, as an individual approaches retirement years, he will first retire part time, and eventually become fully retired because higher income from nonwork sources comes with declining productive power.

The method of calculating the welfare tax advocated here would virtually exclude valuable part-time workers from the labor force because the tax takes income from the initial hours of work at a 100 percent rate.

The problem is relatively minor, but in need of attention for a $1,000 demogrant. But the $2,500 demogrant takes more than a half-year's earnings when calculated full time earnings exceed $5,000. This could be all of the income from even highly paid earners who only wish to work part time.

A tax would certainly discourage valuable work that such a person wished to perform. Nobody benefits from that.

Provisions would have to be made to take care of this situation. A possible device would be to establish official part-time status and to pay on a proportional part of hours worked. This has the disadvantages associated with all categorical programs. Another approach is to reduce the calculated wage rate by placing actual earnings on a 2,000 hour base. The welfare tax would be calculated on that lower potential annual income. Thus a person who actually earns $10 an hour but works only half-time would be treated as if he earned only $5 an hour for welfare tax purposes. This would also require administrative determination.

Summary

The purpose of this chapter is to face some of the practical problems that must be worked out if actual policies based on the analysis of chapters 4 and 5 are to replace the Keynesian-style policies which may have outlived their usefulness. These matters include the size of the demogrant, the method whereby it can be financed, and the effect of the combined demogrant-welfare tax upon the incentives to work offered people in different economic situations.

All analysis is related to individuals, not families. A husband and wife living together with whatever number of children would separately receive the demogrant and separately be subject to the welfare tax.

The welfare tax applies to all income, both from labor and from property. It does not apply to the demogrant. Income from nonlabor sources is taxed as full-time income as if it were received as so much an hour for 2,000 hours. Income from labor is taxed so as to leave untaxed income earned in the actual range of annual hours worked.

Lower income individuals are expected to work less than they do now, and higher income individuals more. The combined effect on total value of output is not estimated. There is reason to believe that the total satisfaction of the population will increase, whatever the effect on the output of goods and services in the market sector.

A TRIAL PROGRAM

It is not feasible to adopt wholesale so costly a program as the one advanced in this book, especially since it calls for a major change of direction. There is no need to do so. Beneficiaries of existing programs such as general assistance and unemployment compensation in particular states, or OASI at the federal level, can be given the option of utilizing their benefits in the manner described in Chapter 5. Firms can enter the program on a voluntary basis. Financing can continue for a time from existing sources. Extensions to increasing numbers of people can follow if the results are favorable.

7

Impacts of Optimal Employment Policy on Government Regulation of Enterprise

This final chapter briefly investigates some of the reasons why demogrant-welfare tax systems may be able to liberate government policy from many costly programs which have had questionable success. We begin by examining the duties of government which lead it to attempt to provide security for individuals by making specific regions, industries, or even firms economically secure. Then we attempt to show that a demogrant-welfare tax system offers more reliable security to individuals and, as a result, may replace the shortcomings of the present system with incentives that more nearly harmonize economic activities and can thereby reduce the contest of pressure groups for special favors.

No effort is made even to list all of the governmental programs that might be affected or displaced. Nor is one singled out for special analysis.

Basic Problem

There is a dilemma involved in public policy toward business. On one hand, even a laissez-faire government *has* to be primarily interested in business. The definition and enforcement of property rights, contractual arrangements, and the provision of security are essential for the production of food, housing, clothing, medical services, and all else that makes life possible, interesting and satisfying. The physical protection of the producers and provisions for orderly work are essential to the survival of a modern society.

Motivation to do one's best is also indispensable. Individuals must value their jobs and make the most of them. Nevertheless, every government must be prepared to let particular firms and industries become extinct as conditions change. Strong motivation to continue uses of resources in established ways must not block more efficient new ways. This creates a dilemma. Short-run security can be achieved if existing ways are protected, but only at the cost of longer term benefits. And it is important that both the innovators and the defenders be motivated to make the most of their resources. If firms, even industries, are to be efficient enough (i.e., are to use the world's resources to serve mankind's needs well enough) to survive, workers and management must value their jobs. They must be willing to work hard, to accept discipline, to continue working when they feel unfairly treated or are disappointed.

Security and motivation are interrelated. Motivation flags unless one can count on enjoying the fruits of labor. The basic meanings of ownership and contract involve reliability of the connection between economic effort and reward. It is therefore entirely natural for government to seek to provide security and motivation by making secure the economic position of particular occupations, industries, and even specific firms. The necessity of such actions appears obvious, especially when the industries produce essential things such as food, communication, or the articles for national defense. Still, even in these industries, government policy often does more harm than good.

Government regulation, subsidy, and special treatment of specific industries often causes economic harm by inhibiting desirable changes.

Desirable changes are inhibited because individuals are encouraged to identify their economic and social well-being with the preservation and expansion of the particular industry, firm, and productive process with which they are familiar. Government authority is often brought to bear by tariffs, licensing, certificates of convenience and necessity, government purchasing policies, and direct regulation of prices and services.

The fact that some groups have been able to use the power of government to better threatened positions, increases the likelihood that a given firm or industry, when threatened by efficient competitors at home or abroad, will utilize their talented executives and important parts of their investment funds to seek favors from government rather than devoting energy to improve their products and processes, or searching for other fields of endeavor where their resources might be more usefully employed.

Special legislation introduced to preserve the livelihoods of individuals in particular occupations often leads to much additional regulation. This is one way it works. If an occupation is made more secure financially, profits, wages, and so on, will tend to rise. People not formerly in the occupation will be attracted to it. This leads to "oversupply" which tends to reduce profits and wages in that industry to the former level. Those who invested recently may suffer serious losses. Both government officials and those in the favored industry see the worsening conditions in the occupation as an inadequacy of government policy rather than a natural result of it. Those who secured the original legislation are likely to feel that the situation can be saved if additional steps are taken by government. A typical move is to limit the "right" to engage in the business to those who have experience, or who have undertaken sufficient training to be able to prove their competence to some official group made up of members of the occupation. Licensing the occupation can accomplish this result. In such ways, government power is utilized to create a monopoly position for a small group of people.

It is obvious that this provides a precedent for nearly every occupation which requires any important amount of training or investment. It should be equally obvious that the benefits, if any, result from the power to exclude.

The power to exclude opens the door for additional, more detailed regulation which intensifies the politization of economic life. Only when some political pressure group, as blacks have recently, find their members excluded, are some of the excluded people able to accomplish what others failed to do—break into the favored business. It is done by securing still more government regulation to open the occupation to their members. One must expect this procedure to encourage still other people to discover some physical, ethnic, or religious trait which can be made into a political weapon to extract some of the monopoly gain.

To summarize: presently, many government programs exist which attempt to provide needed security to individuals by giving aid to the industry or region where they are employed. These programs typically grant some degree of monopoly power or other favors which produce changes which seem to call for additional help and regulation. The assistance given to one industry causes imbalances that affect other industries, and leads them to ask for special favors to match those already granted to some.

One must be skeptical about assertions that all benefit from this system. The gain to one group from favored treatment is eaten away by hundreds of small losses as others receive their favors. There is reason to believe that losses outweigh gains when all obtain favors. A system of universal favoritism is less productive than no favoritism even if the resource cost of the administrative apparatus that utilizes valuable resources to dispense the favors is left out of account. As already noted, the firms divert managerial talent, and funds, that could be used elsewhere, to obtain the favors (which of course are rightly seen as essential to the health of the firm under the circumstances). This diversion of resources further shrinks the useful capacity of the economy.

There are also noneconomic costs. When individuals in government have the ability to favor one industry over another, or one firm over another, they have power. This provides a lucrative opportunity for them. Even honest officials are compromised by the common expectation that they are corrupted. It must be said that if one accepts the desirability of the system, it is possible to defend corruption. But it is not a popular defense. Social discord remains. This system imposes especially high costs on those who are without representation. These often include minority groups, and always include foreigners with whom we trade. In both cases, frustrations and hostility accumulate to be released at intervals in wars and disturbances of shocking apparent irrationality. An example: The United States, like many other nations, has an agriculture program, the object of which is to support farmers' incomes. One of its costs is the ill-will of the Egyptians. The Egyptians made heavy investments to expand cotton production at a time when the United States was supporting cotton prices by purchasing "surplus" cotton and storing it. The fact that it was stored raised world prices. The Egyptian investment was made much less profitable when our "domestic" policy was changed and the cotton sold abroad in large volumes.

Reasons for Government Intervention and Regulation

There are good reasons why the government acts as it does. Present policies are not the result of either ill-will or lack of intelligence. Instead, they are attempts to correct for what economists now call "externalities." Basically, the fact is that when a desirable change occurs, some who are hurt are not adequately compensated. Regulations, subsidies, and the like are sometimes intended to prevent change that causes the uncompensated loss or to redress that balance. The economists' objection is that the interventions are often crude, causing externalities of their own that may be worse than the ones which were to be cured. This is especially true when the effort is directed against dislocations that increase unemployment.

Certainly, one cannot blame a bureaucrat or a senator for feeling that he performs a useful service when he responds to urgent appeals from businesses or labor leaders. Who else is there to inform him of the interests of the productive members of the society whose welfare he is committed to serve? It is not his fault that under present arrangements the economic and social well-being of most people is tied too closely to their holding particular jobs, in particular industries, in particular regions.

Academic economists talk easily of the rise and fall of industries, the mobility of resources, and opportunity costs. "Pressure group economics" seems much more practical to most people. Their conventional wisdom teaches them that economists forget that people find their security, even their purposes in life, as producers of specific goods or services often in their home towns. Protection of these avenues of service, they say, is a prime function of government. Remove that protection and you weaken pride in one's work, undermine motivation, and rot the ties of community. It is easy to see the appeal of pressure group thinking which leads to acceptance of regulation to control change, to plan and manage the economy.

Government Regulation and Control as a Modern Imperative

Government policy toward business has been increasingly interventionist since 1890, and especially so since 1929. Masters of common sense have continually told us that there is an inevitable trend toward government regulation, intervention, and absorption of an increasing proportion of economic activity into publicly owned and managed enterprises.

A declining role for private decision-making is said to be inevitable because of complexity, interdependence, and a growing ability to control from the center. Some social thinkers view a failure to acknowledge these allegedly obvious facts as evidence of mental incapacity, greed, or willful perversion to further the interests of hide-bound traditionalists who are socially blind, emotionally attached to outmoded ways, or financially benefited by freedom from socially desirable controls.

Economists, as a group, tend to be hold-outs against both the conclusion favoring intervention and the reasoning that jumps to it. There are exceptions. It is possible to find well-placed economists, even presidents of the American Economic Association, who believe that greater government intervention is both inevitable and desirable. More will reserve judgment on its desirability, but, viewing it as inevitable, see their practical role as making the regulations as nearly optimal as possible.

The key reason why many believe that ever-increasing governmental intervention is desirable and inevitable is that private decisions will necessarily damage the interests of more and more people (will have externalities) as society becomes more crowded with people and technologically more complex and interdependent. This reason would be without merit if these people did not also believe that government can assemble the necessary information, weigh the consequences intelligently, and devise effective means of action that will in fact improve the situation.

One should wonder a bit about the fact that those favoring government intervention often attribute God-like powers of perception, ability, and good will to "good" leaders, and show impatience with restraints on executive authority, especially the authority of central government. Little evidence is cited to establish the case for superior information, exceptional wisdom, and good will of government authority.

On the contrary, it is easy to fault public authorities. Take, for example, the problem of smoke nuisance, which has recently become prominent. It was analyzed fifty years ago by economists. During that time no government anywhere in the world did much to change the conditions under which the firms operated so as to balance social and private costs. Moreover, government-owned and operated plants continue to be offenders.

It is of interest that when government undertakes an activity which causes damage to some citizen, those damaged generally lose legal recourse to compensation that they have when a private enterprise does the same thing.[1] This is consistent with belief that whatever government does, it advances the public interest, and that whatever is done by private firms or parties is not in the public interest. Legal differences like this reflect an attitude of mind, a prejudice perhaps, but they do nothing to reduce the complexity and interdependence of the economy. What they do is to make it much easier for government authorities to overlook the costs which they impose on others.

The upshot is that government actions which are supposed to make adjustments for past failures of the market mechanism often have very serious external effects of their own. This initial section of this chapter attempts to show what some of them are. Government assistance, especially that which is intended to give people security by granting favors to their industries, is a primary *cause* of the apparent complexity and interdependence which is cited as the reason for additional intervention.

What the Demogrant-Welfare Tax Can Do

A demogrant can help turn policy away from serving a myriad of special interest groups. Support is given to individuals rather than to special groups of producers. Each individual has basic income security and is assisted in finding new ways, if need be, to make a contribution to others. Great benefits can flow from this.

A demogrant system will make a person less dependent upon a specific job for his income. True, it will somewhat weaken his "selfish" motivation for job holding. But it will not eliminate it because the skills and experience relevant to one position are not readily transferred to others. In any case, earned income will usually be a substantial multiple of the demogrant. Moreover, there are significant uncertainties, personal strains, the money costs involved in finding a new position even with a functioning demogrant system that lowers information costs, mobility costs, and employment costs generally.

Nevertheless, the person who is unhappy at his present job can quit more readily because he has the long term security of a demogrant income. The employer will also feel somewhat freer to discharge less suitable employees. The new worker entering the labor force will not feel as unwanted. And the housewife will have a basic income of her own which may properly be cherished as recognition of her useful role in society.

It is too much to say that the top priority for taking a job—its role as a source of personal income—will decline until it falls below its role as an avenue of service to others. The service element, which I believe is important to most people, will, however, rise in relative importance.

The air of desperation that suffuses the pleas for aid to particular groups should be removed. Government policy can be directed less to the preservation of special status for particular groups and industries, and more to an analysis of optimal factor use. One way to state it is that it will reduce the pressure to use government power to advance the interest of one economic group or class at the expense of some other group or class.

This includes foreigners. The obstructions to imports will be softened. The nonsensical and harmful arguments for a minimum wage will be undercut. The case for occupational licensing will be cut down closer to size. The principal basis for the limitation of taxicab numbers by franchise will be severely eroded, as will many other monopoly devices that have dubious effects on the incomes of those who are supposed to be benefited.

A broader point of view discloses a more important change. The *compulsion* to increase production is greatly weakened or eliminated. Under present circumstances it seems to be necessary to expand production in order to maintain employment so as to distribute income to families and to provide a tax base. This is a necessity even if it should happen that much of the output is not much wanted. What other means of distribution is there under present circumstances? What other sources of tax revenue are there with which to finance the necessary programs of government, including the welfare program? This is relevant to the complaint of both militant and resigned ecologists.

The distribution of basic income now depends upon the majority earning it for themselves. Our elaborate welfare system puts great pressure on seeking work if one is healthy and of working age. Our monetary and fiscal policies are designed to provide jobs by increasing productive capacity, and by stimulating total money demand for goods so that the jobs will be available. Paradoxically, it does very little to encourage methods of production that use more labor relative to capital and land. Quite the contrary.

We have tried to show that the problem lies in labor costs that are too high to employers. If that is the root of the difficulty, it will not be overcome by regulations to give advantage to particular groups or by monetary and fiscal policies to expand spending.

We have tried to show that mere stimulation of investment and aggregate demand cannot produce the correct factor price ratios. Instead, the results are production expanded beyond optimal levels, inflation, and continued unemployment.

These conditions are reversed by a demogrant used to place the individual in the labor market, to finance job information and mobility, and to bring the private cost of labor into line with its social cost. The pressure to solve a wide range of social problems by promoting optimal employment is a much more refined goal than full employment. It is feasible when one has a logically tight working definition. As an operational matter, the definition of optimal employment is determined when the size of the demogrant is determined. No one has to work to get sufficient income to support that level of life. From that point the benefits to others are balanced against the costs to the individual. Each individual then becomes virtually able to work the optimum amount as determined by his own preferences which, of course, relate to his capacities to earn and to his condition in life.

Factor price ratios are such as to provide an optimal demand for an optimal supply of labor. There is no need to expand the output of everything in order to expand the demand for labor to some more or less arbitrarily predetermined point. Policy the main goal of which is to "create jobs" is more readily seen for what it is—a waste of resources thought to be necessary to solve an income distribution problem under the circumstances of the moment.

As a consequence of the demogrant, government policy can reach a higher level of rationality. It can make human life less mean and more meaningful.

Notes

Chapter 1
An Unsolved Problem of Modern Economics

1. W. S. and E. S. Woytinsky, *World Population and Production*, New York: Twentieth Century Fund, 1953, p. 436.

2. New York, Harper & Row, p. 69.

3. *Statistical Abstract of the United States*, 1964, table 454, p. 337.

4. Schumpeter, *Capitalism, Socialism, and Democracy*, p. 66.

5. Robert J. Lampman, "Transfer Approaches to Distribution Policy," *American Economic Review,* May 1970, p. 274, presents Mollie Orshansky's data for 1965, which shows only 32.3 percent of the poor receiving "any payment." A larger percentage is covered today. Still omitted are the working poor and many children.

6. "Transfer Approaches to Distribution Policy," p. 271. See also Lampman's *Ends and Means of Reducing Income Poverty*, p. 107 ff., Markham, 1971.

7. *American Economic Review*, March 1972, 62 pp. 1–18.

8. Tobin believes that the concern is grossly out of proportion to the true costs of inflation. Ibid., p. 15.

9. Tobin quite agrees; see ibid., pp. 1–2.

10. Consensus does not exist among economists on this. Tobin believes that unemployment will be reduced permanently by a persistent inflation of 1 to 2 percent a year. Ibid., pp. 9–13. His theory is complex, depending upon the shapes of particular functions, permanent disequilibrium in one set of markets after another, and other special conditions. In general, simpler theories are to be preferred to complex ones.

11. "The Soviet Planning Pendulum," *Problems of Communism* (November–December 1963), p. 21.

Chapter 2
Basis for a Theory of Unemployment

1. These data are calculated from *Handbook of Labor Statistics, 1970*, U.S. Government Printing Office, table 21, pp. 59–60.

Chapter 3
United States Welfare Programs and Work Incentives

1. *Economic Report of the President*, February, 1971, U.S. Superintendent of Documents, table C-20, p. 220.

2. I find that diagrams similar to this one, and others to follow, have previously appeared in the works by Christopher Green, "Negative Taxes and Monetary Incentives to Work: The Static Theory," *Journal of Human Resources*, Summer 1968, 3, 276–79, Richard Perlman, "A Negative Income Tax for Maintaining Work Incentive," *Journal of Human Resources*, Summer 1968, 3, 280–88, Jonathan Kesselman, "Labor-Supply Effects of Income, Income-Work, and Wage Subsidies," *Journal of Human Resources*, Summer 1969, 4, 275–92, Raymond Munts, "Partial Benefit Schedules in Unemployment Insurance: Their Effect on Work Incentive," *Journal of Human Resources,* Spring 1970, 5, 160–76, Hirschel Kasper, "The War on Poverty: A Program for Taxpayers or the Poor?" *Quarterly Review of Economics and Business*, Autumn 1968, 8; 5–28, A. James Heins, "The Welfare Analysis," *Journal of Human Resources,* Summer 1970, 5, 298–303, and Richard Zeckhauser, "Optimal Mechanisms for Income Transfer," *American Economic Review*, June 1971, 61, 324–34.

3. Yale Brozen, "Toward an Ultimate Solution," *Saturday Review*, June 23, 1970, p. 60, paraphrases the conclusions of a relevant study that reveals some of the matters that are involved in the class division. He states, "A study in one community using a matched sample of 16,332 high school students found the incidence of school dropout, juvenile delinquency, poor school discipline, low scholastic aptitude and achievement, and, among girls, teenage marriage and premarital pregnancy, to be consistently higher from AFDC families than among those from matched families with similar income that had never applied for assistance. This was true regardless of whether the families were Negro or White, of high or low socioeconomic status, female or male or jointly-headed. The longer families were on AFDC, the greater the incidence of these problems."

For an intimate account of the effect of unemployment on attitudes see Paul Jacobs, "Unemployment As a Way of Life," ch. 13, A. M. Ross (ed.), *Employment Policy and the Labor Market*, Berkeley, 1965.

4. K. G. Sander, "The Retirement Test: Its Effect on Older Workers' Earnings," *Social Security Bulletin*, June 1968, 31, 3–6.

5. "Partial Benefit Schedules in Unemployment Insurance: Their Effect on Work Incentive," *Journal of Human Resources,* Spring 1970, 5.

6. "Unemployment Insurance, Job Search, and the Demand of Leisure," *Western Economic Journal*, March 1971, 9, 102–7.

7. C. T. Brehm and T. R. Saving, "The Demand for General Assistance Payment," *American Economic Review*, December 1964, 54, 1002–18, and "Reply," *American Economic Review*, June 1967, 57, 585–62.

8. Bruno Stein and P. S. Albin, "The Demand for General Assistance Payments: Comment," *American Economic Review*, June 1967, *57*, 575–84. They cite one study that finds only 1 of 1,300 recipients" might—possibly—be physically able to work," p. 584n.

9. Hirschel Kasper, "Welfare Payments and Work Incentive: Some Determinants of the Rates of General Assistance Payments," *Journal of Human Resources*, Winter 1968, *3*, 86–110.

10. Ibid., pp. 109–10.

11. Yale Brozen, "The Effects of Statutory Minimum Wage Increases on Teenage Unemployment," *Journal of Law and Economics*, April 1969.

12. Lady Juliet Rhys-Williams, *Taxation and Incentive*, New York, 1953.

13. Milton Friedman, *Capitalism and Freedom*, Chicago, 1962.

14. Harold W. Watts, *Mid-Experiment Report on Basic Labor Supply Response*, May, 1971, Institute for Research on Poverty, University of Wisconsin, Madison, May, 1971, "Abstract."

15. Green and Tella, *Effect of Nonemployment Income*, pp. 405ff.

Chapter 4
Individual Decisions and Social Welfare

1. See my "Innovations in the Calculation of Welfare Loss to Monopoly," *Western Economic Journal*, September 1969, 3, 234–43, and "New Estimates of the 'Welfare Loss' to Monopoly: United States, 1956–69," forthcoming.

2. Robert Zechauser believes that typical taxpayers will wish to actively *encourage* useful work, "Optimal Mechanisms for Income Transfer," *American Economic Review*, June 1971, 61, pp. 324–34. On this assumption, he shows that for those capable of working, the optimal arrangement is a negative income guarantee (i.e., a heavy penalty, say a cash fine, levied on those who do not work) supplemented by a substantial subsidy for each dollar earned. Those capable of working can be induced by such a combination to choose to work long hours. This outcome may be deemed optimal in the sense that the average taxpayer gets what he wants (a minimum income for those capable of working and the satisfaction of seeing them at work), and the others get the best that is available to them under the circumstances chosen by the taxpayer.

Zeckhauser points out that this system is applicable only to those capable of working, and acknowledges the need for other welfare programs. Some system, therefore, is still needed to decide who qualifies for each of the various programs, including his tax, wage-subsidy system. A substantial danger remains that many in need will not qualify for any assistance.

The penalty plus wage-subsidy system is essentially punitive. It can force a family to a lower level of satisfaction as compared to what it might enjoy if it could avoid work without the initial penalty. After it has been essentially forced to work the amount that it will find optimal under Zeckhauser's program, its money income may be higher than before, while its welfare may be less.

As presented, Zeckhauser's plan assumes differences of preferences between the typical worker and the typical nonworker which lead the latter not to work for reasons which Zeckhauser does not examine. This is true because it seems from Zeckhauser's presentation that both may have the same earning potential.

3. Stigler, G. J., "Information in the Labor Market," *Journal of Political Economy,* October 1962, Part 2, 70. Alchian, A., "Information Costs, Pricing, and Resource Unemployment," *Western Economic Journal,* June 1969, 7.

4. Axel Leijonhufvud, *On Keynesian Economics and the Economics of Keynes*, Oxford University Press, New York and London, 1968, chapter 5, section 2, p. 335.

5. Donald F. Gordon and Allan Hynes, "On the Theory of Price Dynamics," pp. 369–93, in Edmund S. Phelps, et al., *Microeconomic Foundations of Employment and Inflation Theory*, New York, 1970.

6. For a contrary opinion by a renowned economist, see Tobin's "Inflation and Unemployment," especially pp. 5–13.

Appendix
A Factor Mispricing Theory of Unemployment

1. Harry G. Johnson, "Factor Market Distortions and the Shape of the Transformation Curve," *Econometrica*, July 1966, 34, 686–98.
2. Ibid., p. 687.

Chapter 5
Policies to Equalize Private and Social Costs of Labor

1. "Transfer Approaches to Distribution Policy," *American Economic Review*, May 1970, 60, 276.

Chapter 6
Size of Welfare Payments and Financing

1. *Statistical Abstract for the United States*, 1970, p. 334.

2. Robert J. Lampman, "Transfer Approaches to Distribution Policy," *American Economic Review*, May 1970, 40, 270–79.

3. See Thomas Ireland, *The Economics of Charity*, Center of Public Choice, Blacksburg, Virginia.

4. *Statistical Abstract of the United States*, 1970, p. 8.

5. For a sophisticated treatment of this see Ireland's *Economics of Charity*.

Chapter 7
Impacts of Optimal Employment Policy on Governmental Regulation of Enterprise

1. See Ronald H. Coase, "The Problem of Social Cost," *Journal of Law and Economics,* October 1960, 3, 1–44, for a number of actual cases and a penetrating analysis of the problem.

Index

Aganbegian, A. G., 19–20
  compulsory military service, 19
  criticism of Soviet system, 19–20
  labor turnover, 19–20
  seasonal changes, 19–20
Agricultural manpower, 8
  reduction of, 7
American Economic Association, 142
Amount of human wants, 88
  best solutions, 95–96
  definition of, 88
  Edgeworth Box, 89, 95, 96

Bandiero Rossa (Red Banner) Rome, July, 1956, 19–20

Cobb-Douglas utility function, 32, 34
  illustrated, 33
  "income" and "substitution" effects, 32, 36, 37
Confiscatory policies, 114
  New York City, 114n
Compulsory funding to finance benefits, 116, 126
  illustrated, 124
  lump sum (or property) taxes, 115, 117
Consumer Price Index, 79
Consumption per capita, 7
Council of Economic Advisors, 16, 78

Demogrant-welfare program, 121–136
  advocated for all over 20 years, 100
  aim, 145
  avoidance of special interest groups, 143
  benefits to overall public welfare expense, 131
  capitalized value, 113–114
  combined with welfare tax, 121, 125
  effects on preferences and income opportunities, 102
  illustrated, 124
Distribution of income, 8, 10, 12
  illustrated, 11
Dorodnitsyn, A., 18

Eisenhower, Dwight D., 16

Family Assistance Plan (FAP), 43, 57, 113, 116
  built-in tests, 57
  costs, 57
  illustrated, 59
  wealth and tax effects, 57–60, 77

Federal Reserve System, 17
Ford Motor Company, 7
Full Employment Act of 1948, 16
Full employment optimum, 73
  illustrated, 70
  measure of unemployed manpower, 94
  working definition of, 17

Glushkov (Russian mathematician), 18–19
Government intervention, 16, 139–145
  factor price ratios, 145
  "oversupply", 140
  power of exclusion, 140
  pressure group economics, 142
  subsidy and special treatment, 140
  to extinguish industries, 139
  to protect individuals, firms, industries, 139
  to provide security and motive, 139
Great Depression, 16, 40, 78, 79
Green and Tella data, 26, 28–30, 32–34, 48, 60, 62, 104
  illustrated, 106
  preference curves at stages of life, 105–109
Gross National Product (GNP), 122
  combined demogrant and welfare tax, 125
  illustrated, 119
  OASI, diverse funding of, 125, 126
  relative to household sector, 97
  relative to welfare program cost, 12, 14, 62, 75, 126
  welfare program, 126

Hawthorne effect, 62
  (*See also* Demogrant-welfare plan)
Heder, Walter, 78–79
Hoover, Herbert, 16
"Human capital", 117
  definition of, 117
  government protection of, 118
  value of, 117–118

Income opportunity line, 21–25, 48
  Full-time workers, 122–123
    definition of, 23
    effect of taxes, 25
    hours of work, 25, 28
    illustrated, 24, 27, 29
    "optional" line, 26
    non-work income, 23
    preferences of individuals, 21–22
    size, 23–24

Part-time workers, 137
  hours of work, 25, 38
  indifference curve, 37
  percentage of total output, 137
  preference function, 37
  voluntary group, 23
    size, 23
  welfare tax treatment, 138
Preference function for low-income full-
    time workers, 26
  parallel shift of, 37
  tax effects, 37
  work and non-work income sources, 27–
    28
Income per capita, 7
"Indifference curve", 28, 48
  definition of, 30
  health and responsibilities of worker, 31
  illustrated, 29
  relation to nonwork and work income,
    31
Inflation, 6, 8, 10, 18, 18n

Johnson, Lyndon B., 78–79
Johnson-Savosnick analysis model, 86, 87
Joint Publications Research Service No. 220,
    Sept. 1, 1965, 19

Keynes, J. M., 16, 77–92, 109–110, 138
  analysis and policy, 78–79
  definition of full employment vs. infla-
    tion, 81
  examples, 80
  price rise vs. fall, 82

Mill, John Stuart, 99
Minimal wage legislation, 53–57
  "antieconomic" bias, 57
  illustrated, 41, 56
  relation to employers, 54
  relation to poor, 54
  unemployment rates of teenagers by race,
    55
  teenagers' characteristics, 55
  white and nonwhite employment, 55

National Welfare Rights Organization, 113
New Deal, 16
Nixon, Richard M., 43, 57, 58, 113, 116
Nonwork income, 31, 34, 36
  definition of, 34
  income effect, 36
Norris-LaGuardia Act, 16

Office of Economic Opportunity, 55
Old Age and Survivors Insurance (OASI),
    14, 41, 43–47, 125–126

effect of taxation, 43–47
  funding, 116, 125–126
  illustration of, 41, 44
  introduction of, 14
  (See also Social Security)
Optimal employment, 67, 121, 145
  balance of benefits vs. costs, 145
  competitive model, 67, 68
    alternatives, 67
  harmonization of varying costs, 121
  non-optimal factor pricing, 67n
Optimal life cycle employment, 69
  illustrated, 70
  value of worker's output, 71
Output per capita, 6, 19

Public Assistance, 50–53
  administrative function, 52–53
  generative of a permanent non-productive
    class, 50
  illustrated, 50
  national objective, 53
  "negative tax" effect, 52
  nonwork income complications, 53
  work incentive, 50

Reconstruction Finance Corp., 16

Social Security, 7, 34
  (See Old Age and Survivors Insurance
    (OASI))
Soviet Union, 17–20
  economy, simplicity of, 18
  explanation of full employment, 19
  future planning effort, 19
  unemployment or overemployment, 20
  worker percentages, 19
Stalin, Joseph, 7
Supply Curve of Labor, Barzel and
    McDonald (unpublished), 31–32

Take-home pay, 120
Totalitarian efficiency, 91n, 92
Total welfare program
  definition of, 40
Transfer Approaches to Distribution Policy,
    Lampman, Robert J., 100

Ukrainian Academy of Science, 18–19
Unemployment, 3–108
  benefit payments vs. benefit reductions,
    34
  definitions of, 3, 12, 21, 85, 86, 93, 107,
    108
  illustrated, 89
  imbalance between household and market
    sectors, 86–87, 94–95

in modern specialized society, 14–15
"participation rate", 3
percentage of labor hours, 88
problem of, 3
social pressures, 86
social costs of, 5
subsistence economies, 4
variations of percentages, 7n, 8
  illustrated, 9
world percentages, 4
Unemployment compensation, 8, 48, 72–121
  financing of, 72
  by employer, 72
  by lump sum grant and taxes, 100
  by taxpayers, 73–74
  illustrated, 49, 70, 73
  invitation to fraud, 76
  negative income tax benefits, 77
  private vs. social costs, 74, 75, 100, 121
  public attitudes, 77
United States Bureau of Labor Statistics, 3
United States Census Current Population Survey, 26
  (*See also* Green and Tella)
United States public aid programs (1969), 5
United States Senate Finance Committee, 116

Wage and price controls, 6, 17, 82
  in peacetime conditions, 18
  Soviet Union, 83
  United States, 83

Wage rate, definition of, 69
Welfare programs, 6, 12–14, 99, 113–126
  administrative controls, 40, 63
  class division, 63, 99
  definition of, 39
  expansion of, 6
  funding by state governments, 116
  funding by taxpayers, 116
  growth since World War II, 14
  illustrated, 13, 15
  per capita expense, 12
  share for poor, 114
  tax effects, 37
  total cost, 126
  United States vs. USSR, 115
  workers, by groups, 22
Work incentives, 6, 41–47
  demogrant effects, 127
  effect of taxation, 118
  element of risk, 34, 36
  financing, 133, 135
  illustrated, 128, 130, 133, 135
  income security, 6
  "negative nonwork income", 32
  system of markets, 39
  versatility of labor force, 8
    reasons for, 8, 32
  work disincentives, 40, 41–47
Work income, 34
  illustrated, 35
  influence of welfare programs, 39
  tax effects (reduction of benefits), 36
Workmen's compensation, 7

About the Author

Dean A. Worcester, Jr., Professor at the University of Washington, graduated from the University of Nebraska in 1939 and received his Ph.D. from the University of Minnesota in 1943. He has taught at Louisiana State University, the University of Georgia and the University of the Philippines. His writings include two books, *Fundamentals of Political Economy* (1953) and *Monopoly, Big Business and Welfare in Postwar United States* (1967), and articles in *The American Economic Review, The Journal of Political Economy, The Western Economic Journal, The Journal of Economic Literature, The Journal of Finance, International Social Science Journal, The Philippine Economic Journal* and elsewhere. Several of his articles have been reprinted. Some of his research has been supported by the Ford and Rockefeller Foundations.

Throughout his career he has avoided long-term specialization in any particular branch of economics in the belief that there is a continuing need for generalists who look for ways to bring two or more specialties together.

The author has served as acting chairman of his department and is a recent past president of the Western Economic Association.